FAKE?

LIVING CHRISTLIKE IN A COUNTERFEIT CULTURE

Hester Christensen

©2024 by Hester Christensen. First edition ©2013 by Hester Christensen. All rights reserved. No portion of this book may be reproduced or transmitted in any form or by any means, electronic, mechanical, or print, including photocopying and recording, or by any information storage or retrieval system, except as may be expressly permitted in writing by the author.

Contact Hester at hesterchristensen.com

Cover design: Sam and Shayla McGhee
© 2013. All rights reserved.

Interior design and layout: Sue Hayes Overland

ISBN 9798334798236

Unless otherwise noted Scripture quotations are from The Holy Bible, New International Version, © 1973, 1978, 1984 by the International Bible Society. Zondervan Bible Publishers, Grand Rapids, Michigan. All rights reserved.

Printed in the United States of America 2024

For FAKE? Weekly Teaching Sessions, FAKE? Leader Guide Tools & Tips, and FAKE? Study Resources, please visit author website: www.HesterChristensen.com Discount Code: SAVE20

To my precious Mother, Barbara Jean,
whose walk demonstrated how to love "the least of these,"
whose life beautifully testified to God's redemptive power,
whose death sparked the flames of revival in my soul.
. . . until we meet in the Golden City.

&

To my beloved sisters in Christ,
Cross Trainers Bible Study of Eagle Christian Church 2007-2011,
I will always cherish our years of mining for treasure and ministry together.

Praise for FAKE?

In *FAKE?*, Hester Christensen writes: "It's time to stop playing church." Many of us don't even realize we are faking it. Some of us do, but don't know what to do about it. Hester's study is deep and wide. A participant in this six-week study will not only be able to diagnose the problem, but also discover how to correct it. I highly recommend **FAKE?** to anyone who wants to seek a dynamic and fruitful life as a follower of Christ.

— Carol Stine is an adjunt professor at Boise Bible College in Boise, Idaho. Bachelor's in Christian Ministry from St. Louis Christian College. Author of The Story for Women by Zondervan (electronic edition) in 2011. Carol has partnered in full-time ministry with her husband for over 40 years—20 of them as a missionary in Mexico and more recently the Director of Women's Ministry of Eagle Christian Church for six years.

In *FAKE?* Hester Christensen has succeeded in exposing every possible facet of hypocrisy and Pharisaism that may be lurking in the hearts of us "good" Christians. This study challenges women (and men, too) to do the kind of regular heart examination that insures that our deeds, words, thoughts, and motives are indeed pure, and not phony or artificial. Well researched, and biblically sound, **FAKE?** will help the reader understand why our Lord so severely rebuked the Pharisees and why we must rid ourselves of every trace of Pharisaism.

– Dale Cornett, Professor of Greek and New Testament for 35 years, Boise Bible College, Boise, Idaho. M.A., M.Div., Cincinnati Bible Seminary; B.A., Cincinnati Bible College, Cincinnati, Ohio.

Pharisaism is alive and well in the church and in our own lives. While outwardly zealous for God, we often fail to attend to the smell emanating from our personal white washed tombs. Hester Christensen, in her Bible study ***FAKE?***, tackles this very important issue by helping us understand the tension that existed between Jesus and the Pharisaic faction of Judaism. She not only explores the historical context but also effectively helps us apply that knowledge to our own lives. She writes in style that is easily understood, utilizing personal anecdotes to effectively make her points. It is structured in an easy to follow format that begins by setting the biblical stage and then asks us probing personal questions that help us critique our own performance. I was blessed as I worked through her study because it not only educated me, but forced me to ask myself some difficult questions about my own faith. I highly recommend her Bible study to any person or group interested in exploring this biblical tension both historically and in their everyday lives.

— Dr. Erik Strandness, MD., M.A. Theology, Whitworth University, Spokane, Washington.
Author of *The Director's Cut: Finding God's Screenplay on the Cutting Room Floor.*

Although the Pharisees, as a distinct sect of Judaism, have faded from the stage of history, their spirit still lives on, and those of us who follow Christ can be afflicted by it. In **FAKE?**, Hester Christensen diagnosis' this affliction and prescribes remedies that can liberate your soul. Don't think you suffer from this affliction or need these remedies? Perhaps this study is just for you. Just about all of us can be affected by the spirit of the Pharisees at one time or another and Hester's insight may just help you take off the mask and be more real in your walk with God and relationships with others.

– Dr. John Whittaker, Master's of Divinity, Cincinnati Bible Seminary. Doctorate of Ministry, Gordon Conwell Theological Seminary. Professor for 19 years at Boise Bible College in Boise, Idaho.
Co-Preacher & Adult Education Director for 11 years at New Beginnings Christian Church in Kuna, Idaho. and served as the Teaching Pastor at The Pursuit in Boise, Idaho. Currently produces the Listener's Commentary and leads Bible in Life.

FAKE?: *Living Christlike in a Counterfeit Culture* is a bible study each one of us desperately needs to read. Especially now. Especially today. In a present-day culture that seeks to drive out the very existence of God, Hester Christensen reminds us of the biblical truths we, as Christians, must stand firm upon and live out in our daily lives. I urge every church to use this material in a small group study, just as I invite every Christian to read the beautiful, Scripture-based truths that lie within."

—Jenny Lee Sulpizio, Author of *For the Love of God: A Woman's Guide to Finding Faith and Getting Grace.*

About the Author

Hester has been married to her best friend, David, for twenty-nine years and they have three sons, who are now young adults. She lives in the Pacific Northwest and enjoys the great outdoors with her family and their goldendoodle.

Hester is ordained and has served the local church in pastoral ministry for thirty years with an emphasis in the areas of youth, women, and discipleship ministries. She received her Bachelor's in Christian Education & Bible from Boise Bible College and her Master's in Bible & Theology from Lincoln Christian University.

Hester has been speaking and teaching the Bible for over 25 years. She has impacted many individuals through Bible studies, camps, conferences, retreats, and other events in the United States and abroad. Many people describe her speaking as anointed, authentic, and passionate.

In addition to authoring *FAKE? Living Christlike in a Counterfeit Culture*, a six-week Bible study that includes weekly video teaching, Hester is co-author of *Greater Than a Superhero* and co-author of devotions for Hallmark's mini-series, *When Calls the Heart,* seasons 1-8. In addition, she is a contributing author to several books, written numerous devotions, and has published work featured in several magazines and online sites.

Hester understands how difficult the journey of faith can be. Deeply painful seasons have occurred in her life over the years and the Lord has used them to refine and renew her faith in Him. Her faith journey is a continual work of imperfect progress as she pursues Jesus, becomes more rooted in Him and His Word, and stays engaged in biblical community.

The Lord is molding Hester's heart to be conformed to the image of Jesus and she is grateful. The transforming work of the Holy Spirit is an adventure she believes we all need to keep saying "yes" to! Hester hopes you will join her in embracing the truth of who God is, His heart toward mankind, and how these realities impact our lives.

CONTENTS

INTRODUCTION

Welcome to **FAKE?**: *Living Christlike in a Counterfeit Culture*. I'm so excited for the journey you're about to take over the next six weeks. This study has profoundly impacted me as it is the result of my personal walk with the Lord. Let me share some background to help you better understand my heart and the change the Holy Spirit continues to make in me.

Born and raised in the great state of Oregon, I am number three of six children. My family began to attend church when I was in junior high. In 7th grade, under the influence of my Youth Pastors, I accepted Christ. High school was a struggle as I faced many of the pressures prevalent among teen girls. After graduation I attended Christian College, met and married a Pastor.

My life is a work in progress. I am grateful how the Lord continues to graciously mold my heart to be more like His. When I was younger I wanted to be a 'good' Christian. Masking and covering up sins and insecurities became familiar, out of fear of exposing the true ugliness of my heart. I wanted others to only see the good in me and think I was just fine. I lacked the maturity to be transparent with myself, with God and with others. This continued into adulthood as I struggled to understand what it meant to live a Christian life.

A defining moment came years ago. The Lord used tragedy to catapult Truth into my life. Cancer unexpectedly came and quickly took the life of my dear mother. My heartache led to a season of despair. I wrestled with fundamental core beliefs I held regarding God, death, pain and trials. Comfortable Christianity plagued my need for spiritual maturity. I was too complacent, but this trauma unsettled me.

God's scalpel penetrated my fragile heart through this loss. In time and by the Spirit's conviction, God revealed much to me regarding my heart and relationship with Him. In my brokenness, my soul was laid bare and my heart unzipped.

God tenderly showed me how I compared myself to others, judged people and imposed my agenda on them. I lived and did what was expected of a Christian. Sometimes, the choices I made were for the approval of others and sometimes the motives of my heart were questionable. Pride and legalism were also at the top of His concerns to deal with in my life. My relationship with God did not reflect what He desired. I needed a change of heart, not just behavior.

The condition of my heart will always be the core in my relationship with God. Who I am on the inside is really who I am versus who I may portray on the outside. A heart rightly aligned with Christ loves God and His Word out of devotion not duty; out of love not just a list; out of a relationship not merely abiding by rules. The purity of my external actions will only be as pure as my internal motives.

I forge ahead as I experience the power and work of God in my life. His process of refinement and restoration continues to teach me that my desire should be to give Him all of my heart, not just random pieces. He continues to bring me to a place of humility and freedom in Christ. I have a firmer grasp of His grace and tender mercy. He enables me to see others through the eyes of Christ without judging them.

Now my motivation stems from a deep LOVE for my Savior. He replaces complacency with a passionate pursuit of Him. He sets me free from being a "good" Christian to being a devoted follower. My love for Him is no longer confined to rigidity but rather expressed through an unrestrained heart in wild pursuit of my Savior.

While preparing to deliver my messages for a conference in Boise, Idaho several years ago my key verse was Matthew 5:20, *"For I tell you the truth unless your righteousness surpasses that of the Pharisees and the teachers of the law, you will certainly not enter the kingdom of heaven."* Ouch. This passage penetrated my heart. Weren't they the religious leaders? Didn't they have spiritual knowledge? Why did their righteousness lack kingdom of heaven entrance? God was already purging much from my heart well before this conference but the questions I had regarding this passage of Scripture forced me to evaluate even more the righteousness in my own life.

I knew God was speaking directly to me through this verse and I knew I was witnessing His work in my life beyond anything I had ever experienced. He began to supernaturally exchange my Pharisaical heart of piety to one of purity. As He peeled the layers of hypocrisy away, God led me to share this message with others, knowing that I am not the only woman alive who struggles with these tendencies.

As I combed the New Testament verse by verse, God's Word spoke fresh to me. I began to take meticulous notes on each encounter Christ had with the spiritual leaders in the New Testament. Jesus saved His harshest words of rebuke for the Pharisees and teachers of the law. The very ones who were spiritual leaders neglected to live a life worthy of Christ's praise or Kingdom glory. If Jesus reprimanded the spiritual giants of the first century I knew I better pay attention and heed the warnings Jesus indicted upon these individuals.

It is through faith and obedience to God I share this study with you. May the following pages challenge, encourage and motivate you to live your life fervently in love with **Jesus**; a love that surpasses the obedience required by the Law, but rather a love invigorated by the Holy Spirit and motivated by faith, stemming from His love for you. My prayer for us all is to embrace internal purity over external piety; to live Christlike in a counterfeit culture.

Deep pain and grief birthed this study . . . and I am better for it. I truly am a recovering Pharisee. Although I prayed and prayed for God to heal my mother . . . He, in His infinite and sovereign wisdom chose rather . . . to heal my heart.

With love and gratitude, Hester

VIEWER GUIDE

Genesis 3:6-11

The only covering I need is ____ ____________ ___ ___________ __________.

Masks hide our true ____________. A mask is anything that causes us to pretend and prevents us from living ________________.

Masks cause us to do one or both of two things:

1. We want God or others to think we are ______________ _____ _________.
2. We want God or others to think we aren't ______________ _____ _____.

Sin produces _______ and _________causing us to_________ and _________.

Christ rescues us from our ______.

Christ removes our __________.

Christ restores us into right ________________ ______ ______.

Christ helps us remove our _________.

We can't accurately reflect God until we reject the masks we've grown accustomed to

____________ ___________.

God provided Christ as our ______________ so we can ____________ our guilt and shame, so we can be genuine, so our hearts can become pure.

WEEK ONE

Pharisees and the Law

Day 1

Pharisee Who?

Day 2

Criticized by Christ

Day 3

The Law and Sacrifice

Day 4

The Law and Christ

Day 5

Love Beyond Law

WEEK ONE—PHARISEES AND THE LAW

Day 1: Pharisee Who?

> *"For I tell you that unless your righteousness surpasses that of the Pharisees and the teachers of the law, you will certainly not enter the kingdom of heaven" (Matthew 5:20).*

This Bible verse pierced my heart like a freshly sharpened knife while preparing to teach at a conference in Boise, Idaho. Ouch! My heart was penetrated by the direct, yet gentle, nudge of the Spirit to take some serious inventory in my life. Weren't the Pharisees the religious leaders? Didn't they have spiritual knowledge? Why wasn't their righteousness good enough? God was already purging much from my heart before this event, but the questions I had regarding this passage of Scripture forced me to evaluate, on a deeper gut-wrenching level, my own righteousness and other heart issues in my life.

May the next six weeks be a spiritual journey that will continue to have an impact in our lives for years to come. Are you ready? Set. Let's go!

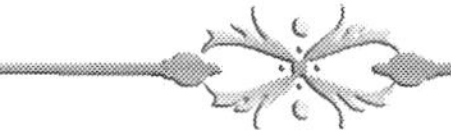

Maybe your perception of a Pharisee stems from the old Sunday school song, *"I don't wanna be a Pharisee . . . I don't wanna be a Pharisee . . . cuz a Pharisee ain't fair, you see . . . I don't wanna be a Pharisee."* [1] We will soon discover there is much more to their lives than being unfair.

An entire study devoted to understanding the Pharisees must adequately inform who they were. A biblical comprehension of their lives is vital to grasp future truths taught throughout this study. Our primary focus will be on the first-century Pharisees, during the time of Christ, even though their roots pre-date Christ.

In addition, we need to obtain a proper understanding of the Law and its purpose. The Pharisees and the Law were partners. How they fit together will provide a clearer picture of truth to be applied through the following lessons.

Today's material will lay the foundation for understanding this group of individuals by covering important historical background information. The name "Pharisee" in its Hebrew form, means the "separated ones or separatists." "It is probable the name was originally coined to reflect the separatists tendencies of these people." [2] They even wore special clothing making them easy to identify. They were also known as highly loyal to God. According to Josephus, a first-century historian, they numbered 6,000 at the pinnacle of their popularity. [3]

1 *"I Just Wanna Be a Sheep." © 1974, 2002. Mission Hills Music. CCLI #454057.*

2 *The Zondervan Encyclopedia of the Bible, Vol 4. Merrill C. Tenney, General Editor, Zondervan, Grand Rapids, MI @2009. p. 843.*

3 *The Zondervan Encyclopedia of the Bible, Vol 4. Merrill C. Tenney, General Editor, Zondervan, Grand Rapids, MI @2009. p. 844.*

The Pharisees were a religious association and functioned as the religious leaders of the Jews. They were also associated with the scribes in interpreting the Law of Moses. In essence, they implemented the religion of the scribes by putting it into practice. Multiple times in the gospels the scribes and Pharisees are mentioned together for this reason.

> *"The Pharisees were not the practical politicians like the more liberal Sadducees, but were the religious leaders of the Jews. The highest qualification for membership was strict adherence to the Law, oral or written."* [4]

There were three distinct societies within Judaism at the time of Christ: The Pharisees, Sadducees, and Essenes. History reveals that the Pharisees were the most influential of the three sects. They were highly revered by the Jewish people, as it was considered an honor to be among them. Not only were they in Jerusalem, but they existed throughout Palestine.

There were three main characteristics that comprised the development of the Pharisees. The first was Jewish legalism. During the Babylonian Captivity in the Old Testament all temple sacrifices and worship had stopped. After their captivity this legalism once again began to spread and follow the prescribed duties of the Jewish Law. Jewish scribes who were closely associated to the Pharisees, combined with the driving force towards legalism, rose to the top in popularity.

The second characteristic defining the development of the Pharisees was their Jewish nationalism. They saw their exile as punishment for neglecting the Law. They believed keeping the Mosaic Law was not only an individual responsibility but also national duty. During the Jews' captivity in the Old Testament, persecution was fierce and attempts to absorb and incorporate the Jews caused them to create an even stronger united front. During this time there was an earnest return to the teachings of the Torah. They did not want to be persuaded by the culture they lived in. It took fierce determination for the Israelites to remain intent in their religious beliefs and refuse to bow their knees to foreign gods. "They strived to remain loyal to their covenant relationship with God which impelled them to resist the increasing pressure toward hellenization [the historical spread of ancient Greek culture]."[5]

The nation of Israel was convicted for prostituting themselves to other nations by worshiping their pagan gods. There is a vast difference between the harlotry God detests and the holiness He desires. Christians today have a constant threat to their covenant relationship with God too. A paramount choice faces us daily: Will we be conformed by culture or transformed by truth? Our culture is saturated with secular beliefs. For example, humanism says, "It's all about me." Pragmatism says, "Whatever works for you." Hedonism says, "Personal pleasure is life's goal - enjoy whatever, whenever, however."

When we allow current culture to determine our beliefs and values, God's truth cannot transform our lives. In order to be transformed by truth we must be conformed to Christ and His Word.

---

4 *Pictorial Bible Dictionary, Merrill C. Tenney. Zondervan Publishing. ©1967, p. 647.*

5 *The Zondervan Encyclopedia of the Bible, Vol 4. Merrill C. Tenney, General Editor, Zondervan, Grand Rapids, MI @2009. p. 843.*

It is vital we know and understand what God's Word teaches because we won't be able to recognize a lie if we don't know the truth. We need to identify false teaching because prevalent myths circulate in our culture. If we're not careful these deceptions will inundate and influence us. They will seek to sabotage our hearts while they secularize our minds. 2 Timothy 4:3-4 instructs about false teaching—what we can expect and what we presently face. This reality should challenge us to be people of the Word of God, carefully examining Scripture like the Bereans in Acts 17:11.

When we embrace the transformative power of God's Word and moral standard of absolute truth, we will be ready, willing and able to reject the world's attempts to conform us to its standards.

Though we may not physically be in captivity like the Israelites, metaphorically we can be captivated by a nation that rejects godly standards and biblical principles. We are in spiritual captivity when we serve cultural gods. On a more personal level, perhaps you live in a non-Christian environment or perhaps your job is a hostile work place for Christians or your children are quieted at school for their beliefs.

> 2 Timothy 4:3-4
>
> *"For the time will come when men will not put up with sound doctrine. Instead, to suit their own desires, they will gather around them a great number of teachers to say what their itching ears want to hear. They will turn their ears away from the truth and turn aside to myths."*

Heart Exam

1. How can Christians collectively implement a stronger united front in the face of the moral degradation we are bombarded with?

2. How can you stand firm without compromising God's standard while witnessing to a lost world?

> Acts 17:11-12
>
> *[11]Now the Bereans were of more noble character than the Thessalonians, for they received the message with great eagerness and examined the Scriptures every day to see if what Paul said was true. [12]Many of the Jews believed, as did also a number of prominent Greek women and many Greek men.*

The third facet to the Pharisees was the growth and maturation of the Jewish religion after their Captivity. This further development of Judaism—along with tradition and the increased separateness—ultimately progressed from its fundamental roots into an expanded form of teaching. This new system of belief added to what was originally taught by the Old Testament Law.

> *"Formulation and adaptation of Mosaic Law by scribe and rabbi, increased tradition and a more extreme separatism resulted in an almost new religion, vehemently opposing all secularization of Judaism by the pagan Greek thought that penetrated Jewish life after the Alexandrian conquest. The Pharisees became a closely organized group, very loyal to the society and to each other, but separate from others, even their own people. They pledged themselves to obey all facets of the traditions to the minutest detail and were sticklers for ceremonial purity."* 6

6 *NIV Compact Dictionary of the Bible, J.D. Douglas & Merrill C. Tenney. Zondervan Publishing. © 1989, p. 454.*

> *"Detailed exposition of the law appeared in the form of innumerable and highly specific injunctions that were designed to "build a hedge" around the written Torah and thus guard against any possible infringement by ignorance or accident. In addition, the new circumstances of the exile and the postexilic period involved matters not covered in the written Torah; consequently, new legislation had to be produced by analogy to, and inference, that which already existed."* [7]

The Pharisees were scrupulous in their compulsive legalism with excessive detail in every area of conduct. "Their behavior was obsessive with regulations handed down by former generations and not recorded in the laws of Moses." [8] Several examples are referenced in the New Testament with "traditions of men, or elders" (Matt. 15 & 23, Mark 7, Luke 11). Traditions that were passed on over the years constituted the "oral law," which started during the Babylonian exile and was highly revered by all. They claimed oral law was equal in authority to Scripture because it tied back to Moses. These laws were continually observed through time—and were even later compiled into what is now called The Mishnah.

"Inevitable weaknesses exist in a system devoted to the formulation of microscopic precepts." [9] More important matters can easily drown in the waters of trivial detail. The Pharisees did not want to unintentionally sin as they adapted to the changing culture. Their intention was protection of their faith in God, but their outcome became perfection, leading to what appeared as a performance-based relationship with God. As we see in Matthew 23:5, *"Everything they do is for men to see."* When performance and perfection are sought, godly motivation ceases, an intimate connection is weakened and personal merit is bought.

3. What modern-day hedges have you built around God's moral law? How could this hedge protect you? How can this hedge encourage perfection and performance?

7 *The Zondervan Encyclopedia of the Bible, Vol 4. Merrill C. Tenney, General Editor, Zondervan, Grand Rapids, MI @2009. p. 846.*

8 *Ibid.*

9 *The Zondervan Encyclopedia of the Bible, Vol 4. Merrill C. Tenney, General Editor, Zondervan, Grand Rapids, MI @2009. p. 848.*

Protection is a good thing, right? Conforming to current culture and/or grieving the Lord by sin should not be a desire of any Christian. The problem comes when we impose our "hedge" on other people's hearts. Or, we force our convictions on their conscience. When these self-imposing mandates become extra-biblical expectation, we run the risk of mishandling Scripture and elevating personal preference to a position of authority. This should not be.

Proper exegesis is necessary when we approach the Word of God—We evaluate and observe Scripture's original context and dissect its interpretation through research: comparing related passages, maintaining respect to grammar and conducting word studies. Then we ask ourselves, what does this mean for us today? What is the application of what we've discovered in the text? Our application of Scripture may vary based on the principles we learn. 2 Timothy 2:15 exhorts us to correctly handle the Word of Truth.

Conformed by culture or transformed by Truth . . .

It's a daily choice.

The Pharisees started with the right intentions. They were highly faithful and devoted to the Law. In time, their teaching and instruction of the Mosaic Law included extensive additions—not established by God—which were expected to be carried out in the lives of the Jewish people. It isn't until the New Testament that a negative picture is painted of the Pharisees. When their path intersected with Christ, bitter opposition arose.

Oh Father, in the midst of the secular culture I live, I ask in faith for Your help to remain grounded in the truth of Your Word. Enable my walk to impact my witness and give me courage to be bold in the face of opposition. May Your Word be deeply rooted in my heart that I can readily recognize deception, extra-biblical teaching and ungodly philosophies.

In Jesus' powerful name I pray,
Amen.

Day 2: Criticized By Christ

Day 2

While Christ criticized the Pharisees collectively, it's unfair to assume all characteristics about all Pharisees were corrupt or that they were all hypocritical and self-righteous. Many of them strived to uphold and advance genuine piety, or devotion to God. The perception we have of Pharisaism from the New Testament is a deteriorated form of authentic Pharisaism.

♡ ***Heart Exam***

1. How do you feel when you hear people say, "Christians are all just a bunch of hypocrites!?" (A hypocrite is a person who pretends to be something they're not. Otherwise known as FAKE.)

This is just the beginning and I'm so glad you started this journey. In the weeks ahead, we will embark on some heart examination and transformation to deepen our personal relationship with Christ.

2. Thinking back, could someone have mistaken you for a hypocrite? If so, what was the situation?

It is pertinent to note, some of the most highly respected men in the New Testament were Pharisees. Nicodemus is mentioned in John 3:1 as one who came to Jesus for further understanding of Christ's teachings. Gamaliel, a Pharisee honored by all the people, addressed the Sanhedrin in Acts 5:34 with a persuasive speech, convincing the men of Israel to not put Peter and the other apostles to death. Joseph of Arimathea (Mark 15:43) a member of the Sanhedrin and a Pharisee, looked for the Kingdom and disagreed to do away with Jesus (Luke 23:51).

> Acts 26:4-5
>
> *[4]The Jews all know the way I have lived ever since I was a child, from the beginning of my life in my own country, and also in Jerusalem. [5]They have known me for a long time and can testify, if they are willing, that according to the strictest sect of our religion, I lived as a Pharisee.*

The apostle Paul is another well-known Pharisee. When he shares his life as a Pharisee in Acts 26:5, he is not condemning what they stood for, but rather expressing it as an honor. For the most part Pharisees were venerated with deep admiration by the people. In Philippians 3:5 when Paul shares his credentials as a Pharisee, he is not considering himself a hypocrite, but preferably showing his faithfulness to the highest standard of the law.

The purpose of this study is to focus on the Pharisees as a whole, during the time of Christ. The evidence shows that New Testament Pharisaism became depraved. In the following weeks as we unpack specific encounters Jesus had with the Pharisees, we will see Christ's harsh condemnation as He addresses their many discrepancies centering on incorrect theology and the condition of their hearts.

> *"The Pharisees despised those whom they did not consider their equals and were haughty and arrogant because they believed they were the only interpreters of God and His Word. It is only natural that ultimately such a religion became only a matter of externals and not of the heart, and that God's grace was thought to come only from doing the Law."* [1]

Bitter opposition arose between Jesus and the Pharisees. The foremost doctrinal dispute was their pursuit of a works-based righteousness which contrasted Jesus' teaching of the *free* gift of salvation, by God's grace, through His death and resurrection.

In short, the Pharisees' hearts spewed legalism, arrogance and self–righteousness. They were judgmental and hypocritical with no shame or remorse. They were loveless, full of greed and elevated external piety. When Christ admonished their severe wickedness they refused any admission of guilt.

The Pharisees' anger towards Christ heightened to where they sought opportunity to trap Him in word and deed in hopes of putting Him to death. They appeared to have it all together externally, but rejected Christ's teachings and ultimately refused to accept Him as the Messiah.

Read Luke 7:18-35

Jesus addresses a crowd of people and explains how John the Baptist came to prepare the way for the Lord. But the Pharisees would not comply with John's teaching. Luke 7:30 states, *"The Pharisees and experts in the law rejected God's purpose for themselves because they had not been baptized by John."*

John preached a baptism of repentance. God's will was for the people of Judea to repent at John's teaching, be baptized and believe in Jesus Christ, Who was to follow. The Pharisees did not obey John nor did they produce the fruit of repentance. However, the Gentile sinners, as noted in verse 29, did acknowledge God's will and followed through with obedient action.

By frustrating God's will and counsel, those who did not accept John's testimony concerning Christ, namely the Pharisees, forfeited the grace of God. Even though they witnessed others accept John's teaching they still scorned such directives. Our condemnation, as is theirs, will be great if we too do not repent, accept Christ and embrace God's will for our lives.

In reference to this passage, the religious leaders taking their place in the Sanhedrin are like children playing in the market. They are no more influenced by the issues of their salvation than silly children singing a song. Jesus weighs the concern over the spiritual nature of our souls as a serious matter.

Jesus closes this section with verse 35, *"But wisdom is proved right by all her children."* The sister passage to this is found in Matthew 11:16-19 where the word "children" is exchanged for "actions." Thus, good actions are the children of wisdom. The result of our actions to Christ's admonition is proven by the folly or wisdom of our choices.

1 *Pictorial Bible Dictionary, Merrill C. Tenney. Zondervan Publishers. ©1967, p. 647.*

♡ Heart Exam

Our spiritual growth and further intimacy with Christ depends on our responses to the following questions: Have you accepted Jesus Christ as your Lord? Are you prepared for how God may address gaping holes in your heart and your relationship with Him through this study? God loves you so much and His death on the cross testifies to this. If you're unsure at this point how to answer these questions, ask Him to help you embrace His truth and humbly accept His instruction instead of resisting His teaching and correction like the Pharisees did.

3. Of the short list mentioned (legalism, arrogance, self-righteousness etc.), briefly list the areas you identify with in your life.

4. Consider Luke 7:31 and ask yourself, *"To what, then, can Jesus compare the people of this generation?"*

5. Write a personal prayer asking God to specifically help you confront these areas and ask for His power and strength to help you overcome these struggles.

Day 3: The Law and Sacrifice

This next section is not intended to be an exhaustive look at the Old Testament Law. The entirety of the Law is beyond the scope of these pages. For the purposes of this study the following text is a general overview of the Law in hopes that we will gain greater awareness and comprehension of its intent.

> *"Judaism separates the Old Testament into three categories: The Law, the Prophets and the Writings. The Greek meaning of the Hebrew word 'torah' is referenced as the Pentateuch and is also known as The Law. Torah means God's instructions or teaching to Israel. The Pentateuch is the first five books of the Bible: Genesis, Exodus, Leviticus, Numbers and Deuteronomy."* [1]

Understanding the history of the Pharisees cannot be complete without further comprehension of the Old Testament Law. Their way of life was embedded in the strict adherence to this Jewish moral code. The Law was established in the Old Testament by Moses after he delivered the Israelites from bondage to the Egyptians and is also identified as the Mosaic Law.

Specific regulations were required for the nation of Israel to abide by to remain morally pure, reflect God's holy nature and maintain right standing in their relationship with God. Egypt did not serve Yahweh, the Israelite God, and corrupted them while in slavery for over 400 years. The Israelites desperately needed to be taught how to maintain their relationship with God and how to demonstrate their obedience and faith in Him. Much of God's instructions for this purpose are recorded in the book of Leviticus.

The Law gave instructions for the people of Israel in how they should live and conduct themselves to the minutest detail. Regulations for clean and unclean meat, Sabbath restrictions, rituals for purification when one became unclean or had an infectious skin disease, codes for cleanliness, unlawful sexual relations, cleansing from mildew, discharges causing uncleanness, punishment for sin, rules for the priests and unacceptable sacrifices are just a few examples covered.

All of these commands were for the express purpose of the Israelites reflecting God's holiness. He wanted them to ***"Be holy because I am holy"*** (Leviticus 19:2). Israel often succumbed to the nations surrounding them, following their pagan practices rather than God's righteous decrees. God insisted they were not to be like the other nations regardless of what the other nations were doing (Leviticus 18:3-4).

It was impossible for the Jewish people to live out every detail and letter of the Law. For them to break *any* part of the Law was to be guilty of breaking all of it (James 2:10). They were bound to sin because of their sinful nature. God is holy and just. In His justice there is a penalty and payment required for sin. They needed their sin atoned for to be made right with God; a ransom price to cover their offenses. Forgiveness came through atonement. Atonement came through blood. Blood came through death.

---

1 *Harper's Bible Dictionary, Paul J. Achtemeier. Harper San Francisco Publishers. ©1985, p. 769, 783 & 1083.*

Day 3

Read Leviticus 4

Because of people's sinful nature and their inability to offer full payment, restitution was established through animal sacrifices. God's purpose for sacrifices was to show the Jewish nation their sinfulness, their need for atonement and that He would accept a substitute for their sins. These sacrifices taught Israel that their relationship with God was not maintained on the basis of their own right standing but by the blood of animals being shed in their place. Only through death and the spilling of blood could the people be cleared of their sins. Life is in the blood (Leviticus 17:11). *"The disposal of blood validated the sacrifice and distinguished the sacrifice from mere slaughter."* [2]

Other sin offerings took place whenever someone unintentionally sinned (Leviticus 4:1,13, 22, 27). When sin was brought to one's attention in the Israelite community—whether Priest, leader or member—he would then bring an unblemished male or female goat or young bull to offer as a worthy sacrifice presentable to the Lord. The offender would lay hands on the head of the animal and then slaughter it. The priest would take a portion of the blood and sprinkle it before the Lord on the horns of the altar and pour the rest at the base of the altar. After removing the animal fat the priest would finally burn the offering on the altar of burnt offering. In addition to cleansing the sanctuary, this act was God's provision for forgiveness of sin, the sin bearer's atonement (Leviticus 4:20, 26, 31, 35).

"Old Testament sacrifices were more than a reminder that accidental wrongs have consequences. They were given in anticipation that God in His grace would provide atonement even for wrongs we didn't realize we were doing. He did this through the death of Christ."

Dennis Fisher—Our Daily Bread, RBC Ministries, Feb 8, 2014.

Read Leviticus 16

God set aside a special day once a year for the complete covering of Israel's sin (Leviticus 16:16). This atonement cleansed and consecrated the Most Holy Place, the Tent of Meeting, the altar, the priests and all the people of the community (Leviticus 16:20, 33). *"On this day atonement will be made for you, to cleanse you. Then, before the Lord, you will be clean from all your sins"* (Leviticus 16:30-31).

On the Day of Atonement, and only then, the High Priest entered the Holy of Holies in the Tabernacle, and eventually the Temple when it was later built in Jerusalem. The Holy of Holies was where the ark of the covenant was placed and where God's presence resided. Two sin offerings were made on this day: one for the priest and one for the community of Israel.

God acquitted the sins of the nation of Israel, for an entire year, through the sacrifice of a goat for a sin offering then sprinkling its blood on the altar of the Lord. This sacrificial act rolled the sins of the people ahead into the next year—when the High Priest would perform the ritual again for the following year. This atonement covered their sin and put them in right standing with God until the next Day of Atonement. Also known as Yom

2 *Ibid, p. 1143-1145.*

Kippur, this celebration was a lasting ordinance for the people of Israel and was expected to be performed annually.

Day 4

In addition, the priest would lay hands on the head of another goat, confess all the rebellion of Israel over it, thus transferring all their sins onto the goat—and then send it into the wilderness. This scape-goat foreshadowed the coming of Christ as the promised sin bearer of all people who would ultimately take upon Himself the sins of mankind at the cross.

Read Hebrews 10:1-18

Heart Exam

1. In light of what we have learned regarding the Law, what does, *"The law is only a shadow of the good things to come,"* mean in verse 1? What better things than the Law would come? Why is this important for us today?

2. According to verses 1-4, 11, why were annual sacrifices necessary? What were the animal sacrifices unable to accomplish?

3. Verses 7 and 10 speak of God's will. What was God's will for Christ? What was the result for us, the recipients of God's will (vv. 10, 14)? Why is this significant?

Hebrews 10:1-4

[1]The law is only a shadow of the good things that are coming–not the realities themselves. For this reason it can never, by the same sacrifices repeated endlessly year after year, make perfect those who draw near to worship. [2]If it could, would they not have stopped being offered? For the worshipers would have been cleansed once for all, and would no longer have felt guilty for their sins. [3]But those sacrifices are an annual reminder of sins, [4]because it is impossible for the blood of bulls and goats to take away sins.

4. Compare and contrast the *"once for all"* payment of Christ's sacrifice (v. 10) and the *"day after day . . . again and again"* sacrifices the priest performed (v. 11). "Once for all" is like the preamble to the Christian Constitution. How are these three words monumental to our faith? (Also cross reference Hebrews 7:27; 9:25-28)

5. According to Hebrews 10:15-18, what is the covenant the Holy Spirit testifies He will make with us? There are four specific results of this covenant. How does this contrast to the Old Testament Law?

This passage comes from Jeremiah 31:33. *God will put His laws in our hearts and on our minds. Where sins are forgiven there is no longer any need for sacrifices.* There is more to come on this passage in Day 5. Spend time reflecting on what you've gleaned from Scripture thus far and the ultimate sacrifice for sin.

Day 4: The Law and Christ

Day 4

The Law condemns everyone because no one can keep it perfectly. God put it into effect because of sin (Galatians 3:19). The Law's purpose was to allow man to recognize his sin (Romans 3:20), in order to acknowledge his need for Christ. Galatians 3:24-25 says, *"So the law was put in charge to lead us to Christ that we might be justified by faith. Now that faith has come, we are no longer under the supervision of the law."*

> *Romans 7:4, 6*
>
> *[4]So, my brothers, you also died to the law through the body of Christ, that you might belong to another, to him who was raised from the dead, in order that we might bear fruit to God. [6]But now, by dying to what once bound us, we have been released from the law so that we serve in the new way of the Spirit, and not in the old way of the written code.*

Unlike the annual Day of Atonement, Christ's sacrifice paid the ransom once for all, for all people's sin. No more rolling man's sins ahead through animal sacrifices, burnt offerings and sin offerings. The old order of Law and sacrifices was abolished through His death (Ephesians 2:15a). There was no longer need for the High Priest to offer regular sacrifices. Christ was the perfect unblemished sacrifice for all mankind. Christ's atonement also abolished the levitical requirements, food rules and Sabbath guidelines for righteousness and living.

When Christ died, the veil in the Temple was torn in two, signifying we are now under a new covenant; a covenant of grace through faith and not of Law. In addition, the tearing of the veil opened direct access to God, who was now available to all. We have no need of a high priest to go before God on our behalf. Jesus is our High Priest, Who went before us to the cross.

What the Old Testament Law and sacrifices could not do, Christ's death accomplished (Romans 8:3-4). The Law could not impart life (Galatians 3:21). The Law could not impart righteousness (Galatians 3:21). The Law held us as prisoners of sin (Galatians 3:22-23). The Law kept us under a curse (Galatians 3:10, 13). Christ lived a perfectly sinless life adhering to the Old Testament Law. His life became our sin offering to extend forgiveness of sin and salvation for those who accept His sacrifice by faith as payment.

> *Romans 6:11-14*
>
> *[11]In the same way, count yourselves dead to sin but alive to God in Christ Jesus.*
> *[12]Therefore do not let sin reign in your mortal body so that you obey its evil desires. [13]Do not offer the parts of your body to sin, as instruments of wickedness, but rather offer yourselves to God, as those who have been brought from death to life; and offer the parts of your body to him as instruments of righteousness. [14]For sin shall not be your master, because you are not under law, but under grace.*

Romans 3 and 4 teaches us righteousness comes by faith in Christ, not through the Law (3:20, 28; 4:13). Paul uses Abraham as an example proving that *"Abraham believed God, and it was credited to him as righteousness"* (Romans 4:3). A few verses later he shows that Abraham's faith was credited to him while he was still uncircumcised, which renounces the idea that Abraham performed some work to receive this righteousness. The closing verses of Romans 4 are critical: *"The words 'it was credited to him [Abraham],' were written not for him alone, but also for us, to whom God will credit righteousness-for us who believe in Him who raised Jesus our Lord from the dead. He was delivered over to death for our sins and was raised to life for our justification"* (Romans 4:23-25).

Even in the Old Testament, faith was the foundation, not the Law, which justified a person before God. Faith has always been how God counts people righteous. Romans 4:16 reminds us that the promise comes through faith, so that it might be by grace. *"What was promised, being given through faith in Jesus Christ, might be given to those who believe"* (Galatians 3:22b). Through God's unmerited favor—not our striving or working—can we accept by faith the sacrifice of Christ to cover our sin. Galatians 3:11 loudly resounds, *"Clearly no one is justified before God by the law, because, 'The righteous will live by faith.' "*

Day 4

The Old Testament Law pointed to Christ in the New Testament as the complete fulfillment of the Law. The Old Testament ceremonies and rituals were symbolic and represented a new present reality made through Christ. The Messiah had been predicted for hundreds of years and the time came (Isaiah 9:6-7; 53). The prophecies of Christ predict Him as the solution to mankind's problem of sin. Upon Jesus' death, this new teaching of faith in Christ—death to the Law—was embraced by Jesus' disciples yet rejected by the Pharisees and teachers of the Law (Romans 7:4, 6). Even though they knew it was foretold, they refused to accept Jesus as the Anointed One.

For years and years strict adherence to the Law was the Israelites' way of life. Over and over they repeated the rituals governing their lives, purity and relationship with God. Each stroke of the hammer embedded the written code into Christ's cross. His blood covered and cleansed the shortcomings of the Law, granting us His grace and justification by faith in Him. His nail-pierced flesh releases us to live beyond our own toil, to receive His forgiveness, embrace His freedom and walk according to His Spirit—the promise that came through Abraham (Galatians 3:14).

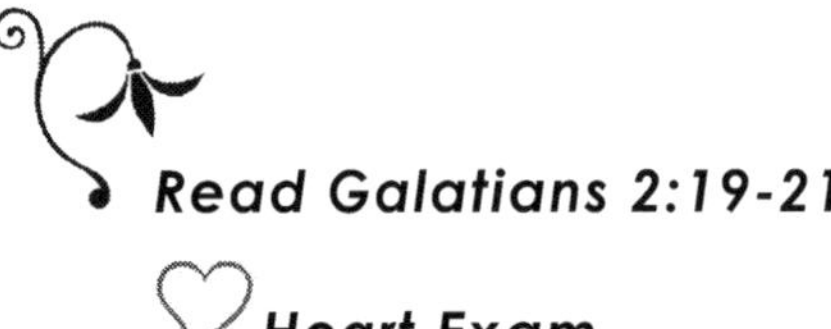

Read Galatians 2:19-21

Heart Exam

1. According to verse 19, how can we live for God?

According to verse 20 we are crucified with Christ. We no longer live, but Christ lives in us. Cross reference Romans 6:6 and 2 Corinthians 4:10-12.

2. How does Christ live in you and what does this look like in your life today? (Reference Galatians 2:20 and read Romans 6:11-14). Be specific. How does this death really bring life?

3. According to Galatians 2:21, how might we be setting aside the grace of God? Why was Christ's sacrifice necessary?

4. How is faith an intricate part of our righteousness and salvation? (Cross reference Galatians 3:9, 11-12, 23 and Romans 4:24-25)

Here we are, living under the new covenant of God's grace and mercy through Christ, yet some still live as though they are yoked to the Law, striving to earn their goodness and righteousness by human effort. The Israelites elevated the Law above the truth of Christ which inhibited their embrace of justification by faith. We must acknowledge we are saved by grace through faith in Christ Jesus. Calvary was inherently the greatest Day of Atonement for mankind. [1]

> *"Even if they had accomplished what they theoretically set out to do in successfully living according to a reformed oral tradition, they had no claim upon God. Merit before God on the basis of righteous works is a nonentity, and thus the whole Pharisaic outlook was vitiated [impaired and weakened] by this basic deception."* [2]

1 *NIV Compact Dictionary of the Bible, J.D. Douglas & Merrill C. Tenney. Zondervan Publishers, © 1989 p. 60.*

2 *The Zondervan Encyclopedia of the Bible, Vol 4. Merrill C. Tenney, General Editor, Zondervan, Grand Rapids, MI @2009. p. 851.*

Day 5

Day 5: Love Beyond Law

"Love the Lord your God with all your heart and with all your soul and with all your strength. These commandments that I give you today are to be upon your hearts" (Deuteronomy 6:5-6). Moses delivered this message shortly after issuing the Israelites the Ten Commandments. Their charge was to love God above and beyond anything with every part of their very being. The degree of their love was revealed by their obedience to Him, or lack thereof.

Just as the Israelites needed to be taught right from wrong, so do we. When the law is broken, sin is revealed. Without the law we wouldn't even know we have sinned against the Lord. Similar to instructing our children from infancy, we all need proper guidelines to understand when we've crossed the line. When we mature as children we also learn there are consequences for our choices.

As a parent, I certainly desire for my children to obey me because they love and respect me and don't want to disappoint me, not because *"I'm Mom and I said so."* Parents don't want their children to begrudgingly perform a task because they "have to." A heart disconnected from love will not experience the 'want to' stemming from internal pure motivation. Unfortunately, there are times when I have to exercise my authority as their Mom. I strive to shepherd their hearts and desire joyful obedience—not forced out of obligation. Sadly, this isn't always the case. Their choice to honor me through obedience is an accurate measure of their love for me as their parent and reveals the condition of their hearts.

God established the Law and sacrifices to lead the people into right living and to honor Him as their Lord. In addition to blood sacrifices, as mentioned earlier, there were sacrifices and offerings that were not from animals—such as the grain offering or drink offering. Sacrifices and offerings were part of the covenant between Israel and Jehovah. The foundational principle was obedience, not sacrifice. Sacrifices were aids to obedience. Without obedience and faith, the offerings were valueless. [3]

> *Mark 12:33*
>
> *33 To love him with all your heart, with all your understanding and with all your strength, and to love your neighbor as yourself is more important than all burnt offerings and sacrifices.*

What started out as a vital component to the Israelites' worship of God lost sight of a heart truly devoted to Him. Through time the Israelites' external actions became disconnected from their internal temperature. They may have performed the right exercises outwardly, but their hearts became calloused, expressing a ritualistic mindset. Love was missing. Outward obedience, without love, is empty.

Read Isaiah 1:11-17

. . . and complete the Heart Exam on the following page.

3 *Pictorial Bible Dictionary, Merrill C. Tenney. Zondervan Publishers. © 1967, p. 602 & p. 738.*

Heart Exam

1. These verses reveal a lot about the Israelites' sacrifices. How does God describe the religious ceremonies? What will happen to their prayers? What does God tell them to do instead?

Read Amos 5:21-27

2. God says He hates and despises the Israelites' religious feasts and sacrifices. What is God's response to their external displays? According to verse 26 what were the consequences when the Israelites elevated and worshiped other gods?

Read Mark 12:33

3. How are we to love God according to this verse? How are we to love others?

4. What is this love more important than? Hopefully we are starting to see a connection between sacrifices and a heart that loves God and others as He desires. What is the contrast Jesus is making?

Day 5

King David laments over his grievous sin and writes a Psalm to God expressing his sorrow. Psalm 51:16-17 declares, *"You do not delight in sacrifice, or I would bring it; you do not take pleasure in burnt offerings. The sacrifices of God are a broken spirit; a broken and contrite heart, O God, you will not despise."* Later Hosea confronts Israel's sin toward God and addresses their lack of repentance. Hosea 6:6 reveals, *"For I desire mercy, not sacrifice, and acknowledgment of God rather than burnt offerings." Proverbs 21:3 also shows us, "To do what is right and just is more acceptable to the Lord than sacrifice."*

From these verses, five attributes are mentioned that God delights in: A broken spirit, a contrite heart, mercy, acknowledgment of God and to do what is right and just. The very sacrifices that had been an expression of love, repentance and worship, no longer pleased God. Scripture reveals He actually despised them. Israelites had the external measurement of rightness through their sacrifices, but they lacked the internal measurement of purity and obedience.

> *"A contrite heart is a heart that is broken to pieces, metaphorically. In Scripture, the heart is the seat of all feeling and emotion, whether joy or sorrow. A contrite heart is one in which pride and self-sufficiency have been completely humbled by the consciousness of guilt. The theological term "contrition" refers to the grief experienced as a consequence of the revelation of sin."* [4]

David experienced contrition after the prophet Nathan confronted his sin. His expression is seen throughout Psalm 51. He acknowledges God's greater desire for believers to offer Him a humble heart that recognizes one's sin and acknowledges the supremacy of God.

This principle is also seen in the New Testament when Paul writes the Romans. Chapter 12:1 exhorts us, *"Therefore, I urge you, brothers, in view of God's mercy, to offer your bodies as living sacrifices, holy and pleasing to God - this is your spiritual act of worship."* A living sacrifice. Really? Certainly the Jewish audience Paul is writing to knew all about Old Testament sacrifices. Paul is teaching that we are to sacrifice ourselves on the altar of Christ. To sacrifice something means something dies. When we submit to God by dying to ourselves, we sacrifice our will to His will. Our spiritual act of worship is to give our hearts to God and allow His governance over us. Ultimately we cannot have this broken and contrite spirit David speaks of until we willingly sacrifice our lives for Him.

People can perform the right "acts" and do the right "things" but unless the heart is connected to the action, they are void of an expression of faith or love. God didn't want the people's sacrifices; He wanted their hearts. He desired an internal motivation of genuine love for Him that stemmed from a broken spirit and contrite heart. God knows this compatible duo will readily acknowledge Him.

Jeremiah 31:33 declares, *"This is the covenant I will make with the house of Israel after that time," declares the Lord. "I will put my law in their minds and write it on their hearts. I will be their God, and they will be my people."*

---

4 *International Standard Bible Encyclopedia, H. E. Jacobs. http://www.blueletterbible.org/search/Dictionary/viewTopic.cfm?topic=IT0002297 (accessed 1-28-13).*

God says He will establish a new covenant with the house of Israel and Judah. Prior verse 32 reveals it will be unlike the covenant He made with them when He led them out of Egypt. While God was faithful, Israel broke their covenant with God. God established a new covenant, not a new law, through Christ. Christ didn't come to destroy the Mosaic Law; Christ came to fulfill the Law. The prophecy Jeremiah declared referenced a future time when Israel would follow God's Law, not because it was chiseled on stone, but rather, because God's Spirit penetrated divine moral law on people's hearts and minds.

Even Solomon understood this concept when he penned Proverbs 3:3, *"Let love and faithfulness never leave you; bind them around your neck, write them on the tablet of your heart."* When God's commands remain on stone they never enter our souls. When they are in our hearts they are expressed through the very fiber of our being and ultimately become who we are.

The Israelites had God's Laws on tablets of stone. Periodically, they entered the lives of people and were expressed through a heart of devotion. Similarly today, we possess God's written Word on sheets of paper. The great paradox is to understand how to get these moral laws and commands off the physical, where they are written, and into the metaphysical, where motivation to live out God's law stems from genuine love by faith in the Spirit.

♡ ***Heart Exam***

5. For you personally, is God's law written on tablets of stone, or on your heart? What is the difference?

6. Maybe you have a little of both mentioned above. What inhibits you from getting your heart right with the Lord?

7. How is it we can have the right external actions, but lack any connection to faith or love? How may you be living with the "right actions" that might be void of faith and love?

Day 5

8. What does God really desire based on what you've studied in Isaiah and Amos today?

God did not say, "*Love the Lord with all your actions . . . or love the Lord with all your external ability.*" He chose four carefully crafted words that communicate a depth of intimacy with Him that cannot be mechanically generated, cannot be wished for, and cannot unequivocally be found or experienced elsewhere. We are to love God . . . "*with all our heart.*" Genuine love produces the fruit of obedience.

Sixty-seven verses in the Bible contain the phrase, ***"All your heart."*** [5] The biblical usage of the word "heart," refers to the seat of affections and implies the innermost being. [6] To love God with all our heart indicates to do so with everything we are, or, all that is within us. This also suggests that to love God with anything less is not enough.

> *"Rules can be observed mechanically. Once they become habitual, they can be followed with minimal effort and almost no thought. These habit-forming rules provide a false sense of security, lulling the soul into a comatose condition."* [7]

The Law governed the Israelites' behavior but could not govern their hearts. Love beyond law is the true antidote for us all. To love God is to be motivated to please Him beyond a prescribed set of rules. Even as we live under the new covenant of grace, our external actions can become rote and lack any connection to genuine love.

God is love and He expressed this sacrificially through Christ's death. How we live reflects our love of God and our obedience to Him. Our response to His love should encourage us to live a life honoring to Him (2 Timothy 1:9). We don't do good things to get saved; we do them because **we are** saved. We were created to do good works because we are God's workmanship (Ephesians 2:10).

5 *http://www.blueletterbible.org/search/search.cfm?Criteria=all+your+heart&t=NASB#s=s_primary_0_1 (accessed 1-28-13).*

6 *http://www.blueletterbible.org/lang/lexicon/lexicon.cfm?Strongs=H3824&t=NASB (accessed 1-28-13).*

7 *Jesus Calling: Enjoying Peace in His Presence, Sarah Young. Thomas Nelson Publishers. © 2004, p. 357.*

Leviticus 17; 4; 11; 16:33; Hebrews 10:4; Romans 3:25; Hebrews 10:1-4; 10-18; John 19:30; Colossians 2:13-14; 1 Peter 1:18; 2:24; Isaiah 53:5; Colossians 2:8

God provided the means for atonement and reconciliation through Old Testament covenant Law by means of the sacrificial system, where the death and ____________of an animal was accepted by God as a __________________ for the offender.

Old Testament sacrifices were inadequate because they did not fully solve the problem of _____ .

Jesus Christ was the final ____ ______________ .

• •

John 19:30

Tetelestai - it is finished.[1] Just as, "once for all," is monumental to our faith, equally vital is "____ ____ ______________ ."

Colossians 2:13-14

Cheirographon – hand written legal document. [2, 3]

• •

We all have a 'Certificate of ________ .' Jesus Christ nailed our ________ to the cross, so no charge can ever come against us.

Our 'Certificate of _______ ,' has been changed to a 'Certificate of __________________ .' We no longer stand condemned . . . we stand ______________ !

1. We cannot save________________ .
2. We are in need of _________________ .
3. Our identity, our worth etc. is only found ___ __________ _________ ____ ____ ______________ _______ ____ _____ _________ !

If these truths are not the foundation we are building on, we will be prone to take confidence in the _________ .

_______ . In. _______ !

WEEK TWO

Internal Purity Versus External Piety

Day 1

When Rites Are Wrong

Day 2

Matters of the Heart

Day 3

Bridging the Gap

Day 4

Resumé Righteousness

Day 5

Uncover the Cover-up

WEEK TWO—INTERNAL PURITY VERSUS EXTERNAL PIETY

Day 1: When Rites Are Wrong

My prayer for Week One was to build a solid foundation in order for the following weeks to springboard off of each other. Having a firmer grasp of the Pharisees enables us to have some background as we dig into various scenes in the New Testament. Understanding what the Law was, its purpose and fulfillment also gives us a proper framework as we encounter the Pharisees and their elevation of the Law, lack of grace and misguided piety. As Week One came to a close, we reviewed the importance of genuine love for God, which is ultimately the core of this study. When we love God with a pure heart, we will follow His instructions with proper motives—not just for the sake of rule keeping.

In Mark 7, Jesus has an encounter with the Pharisees and teachers of religious Law. They were quick to point out a supposed error of Christ's disciples. The fault-finders fussed over externals while gloating over their own ways and goodness. Jesus uses this opportunity to admonish these leaders and teach a valuable lesson about the traditions of men and inward purity.

The Pharisees were not criticizing the disciples' lack of hygiene but rather their disregard for tradition. The Pharisees ask Jesus, *"Why don't your disciples live according to the traditions of the elders?"* But what they were really saying was, *"How come your disciples don't do what we do?"*

Ceremonial hand washing was part of Old Testament Law. It was intended for those who were priests (Exodus 30:19; 40:12). Priests were instructed to be ceremonially clean before entering the tabernacle to perform their religious duties. In Mark 7, we see how the Pharisees have added unnecessary requirements to the Law. They insist on more than the Law required (with cups, kettles and pitchers). They also prescribe washing for circumstances beyond the Law's intent (before a meal). Although the Law commanded it only for the priests, they include the disciples in this ritual. The Pharisees attached their own man-made customs to the Law and expected others to follow them.

> *"The expressed reason for this was the desire for purity. They sought to maintain in their own homes the same state of ritual purity required of the priests in the temple. In their words, they wanted to build a fence around the Law, so that if people didn't cross the boundary of their applications of Scripture (i.e., sacred traditions) they certainly wouldn't break the Law. Perhaps one modern example would be wearing a bikini. What the bible prescribes is modesty; one application is no bikinis. The moment,*

Day 1

however, we confuse our applications with the biblical principles; we are acting very much like the Pharisees. Another example could be daily devotions ... a good suggestion, but not to be equated with the biblical principle of loving Scripture and being devoted to prayer." [1]

♡ Heart Exam

1. Name two traditions the Pharisees abided by before they would eat. What else did they add? Why or why not? Was it necessary for Christ's disciples to follow these rules?

2. Why were the Pharisees' traditions an issue with Jesus? What does Mark 7:6, 8 reveal?

Church traditions can provide stability and familiarity. However, through the ages church traditions have also been elevated to a place of expectancy, rigidity and a prescription for the Christian life.

We all have traditions, but do we realize how tightly we hold onto them and perhaps impose them on others? Do we question others because we think they don't sing the right songs, play the proper kinds of instruments, wear the right clothes, administer communion the right way, read from the right Bible translation, observe the right catechisms, or have the right kind of building? Or vice versa, are we the ones who look down on those who believe there is one proper way to do communion or who believe that God does care about which instruments are used in worship, believing we are on a higher plane? Both are sinful and reveal an immature heart taking confidence in the flesh.

♡ Heart Exam

3. What traditions in the church do people get hung up on today? Think beyond carpet color, worship style and chair preference. (There are a lot!)

1 *Quote by Dr. John Whittaker, Professor of Preaching & New Testament, Boise Bible College, Boise, Idaho. June 28, 2013.*

4. Share any religious traditions you grew up with and any you currently exercise. What positive results or negative outcomes have you experienced with traditions?

5. Are there any traditions you may presently elevate above God's Word? Do you force them on others?

It's necessary we understand our motives for practicing certain traditions. If we're not careful, they can become divisive and turn into idol worship. Many good things can come from them, but when we exchange traditions for flexibility and open-mindedness, we can inhibit grace and true worship of God.

The opposite can also occur. We can dishonor God if we're too open-minded and allow anything. Perhaps we falsely worship traditions over the truth. Regardless of what traditions we hold to, the motives of our hearts reveal the measure of hypocrisy Jesus is addressing in this passage. Sadly, for the Pharisees, their rites became wrong.

Day 2: Matters Of The Heart

We can see from Scripture how traditions can be twisted, touted as truth and expected as the biblical norm for living. Today, we will begin by looking at Jesus' response to the Pharisees' initial question, ***"Why don't your disciples live according to the traditions of the elders?"***

Mark 7:6-7

6He replied, "Isaiah was right when he prophesied about you hypocrites; as it is written: " 'These people honor me with their lips, but their hearts are far from me. 7They worship me in vain; their teachings are but rules taught by men.' "

Jesus doesn't skip a beat. He reveals the hypocrisy in the hearts of the Pharisees by quoting the Word of God. First, the prophet Isaiah indicts false piety. Secondly, Moses, the giver of the Law, exposes a deeper issue of trying to 'legally' violate God's law with a loophole. Let's take a look at the first one.

1. According to Mark 7:6-7, what four specific charges does the prophecy in Isaiah 29:13 make against these people? Why does Jesus declare they are guilty of them?

According to Isaiah's words, I must confess that I have been 'one of these' people. Sadly, there are times when I honor God with my mouth but not with my heart. Or, when my worship is in vain; merely a mechanical expression void of true reverence for our Lord. When this happens, I'm thankful for the conviction of God's Spirit that leads me to repentance and restores my heart. I desire to reflect my love for God more than the Pharisees did. I do **not** want to be "one of these," yet I know the tendency is there for all of us to fall short.

2. How have you been "one of these people?" Be specific.

> *"They honour me with their lips, they pretend it is for the glory of God that they impose those things, to distinguish themselves from the heathen; but really their heart is far from God, and is governed by nothing but ambition and covetousness. They would be thought hereby to appropriate themselves as a holy people to the Lord their God, when really it is the furthest thing in their thought."* [1]

Imagine God saying this prophecy to us. A proper response would be to fall prostrate and evaluate the condition of our hearts. Are they cold, indifferent and complacent, or are our hearts alive, passionate and honoring of Yahweh? Digesting such a rebuke should bring us to our knees in humble repentance. May each of our prayers become, *"Oh Lord, help me to be a person who honors You with my lips and whose heart is close to You. May my worship be a genuine expression of my love. Enable me to resist man-made rituals as a means of righteousness, but rather embrace God's commands."*

---

1 *Commentary on Mark by Matthew Henry. :http://www.blueletterbible.org/commentaries/comm_view.cfm?AuthorID=4&contentID=1631&commInfo=5&topic=Mark (accessed 1-24-2013).*

Heart Exam

Day 2

3. Empty ritual can strip worship of its meaning and power. When is worship in vain? What makes worship genuine?

4. Do you ever feel like you are just going through the motions in regards to your faith? Explain.

Next, we witness Christ giving the Pharisees an example of how they were guilty of overriding the Word of God with their own traditions. Jesus references Exodus 21:17 and 20:12 by reiterating the Law of Moses and how children are to honor their father and mother. We shouldn't assume this reprimand is only for young children, but even more, the Law instructs adult children to care for the needs of their aging parents.

The Pharisees circumvented this command by allowing people to dedicate to the Lord a gift they should have given to their parents. The Pharisees believed it was okay to legally exclude one's parents from a child's obligation, thereby releasing the child from God's command. [2] It's good to give gifts to God, right? Not at the expense of dishonoring His law. When we try to escape God's commands for our own preferences—especially when we try to appear religious while doing so—we are hypocrites. Jesus wraps up this portion of Scripture by declaring that the Pharisees "do many things like that." They were guilty of nullifying the Word of God for their own tradition, not just once, but many times.

The Pharisees taught man-made rules as truth, then expected others to follow suit. Their traditions became "law" to them. They held them in equal authority to God's Word. They even honored these traditions above God's law by forsaking the greater commands of Scripture. Though they were quick to accuse the disciples of wrong, they neglected to see their own disobedience. The Pharisees' hearts betrayed their lips. As a result, their worship of God was a religious show.

We know from Week One, God wants our hearts, not just right actions, and certainly not man-made traditions. He knows our internal make-up and acknowledges the condition of one's heart is the core in a relationship with Him. Internal devotion affects external action. His inner work affects our outlook. The heart is like a thermostat, gauging why we do what we do. It is vital to keep constant awareness of its temperature because of our sinful nature. We must recognize and repent for the sin and struggles we face. Without this restoration we will fail to maintain a heart that is properly aligned with God.

2 *Robertson's Word Pictures of the New Testament. http://classic.studylight.org/com/rwp/view.cgi?-book=mr&chapter=007&verse=011 (accessed 1-31-2013).*

Day 2

Read Mark 7:17-23

After Jesus confronts the Pharisees' neglect of the Word of God and the favoring of their own wisdom, He calls the crowd in closer so He can go deeper in His teaching. Mark 7:15 (NLT) reads, *"It's not what goes into your body that defiles you; you are defiled by what comes from your heart."* He further explains that food doesn't defile us because it doesn't go into our heart. Food goes from the stomach to the sewer; not from the stomach to the soul. This teaching went against the Pharisees because they upheld the Law in which certain foods were considered unclean for consumption. In verse 19, Mark says that Jesus declared all foods acceptable in the eyes of God.

In verse 20, Jesus hammers home His point by denouncing previously held notions. He professes and firmly upholds, *"It is what comes from inside that defiles you."* Or, *"what comes out of man is what makes him 'unclean' "* (NLT). Jesus then lists in the following two verses the things that come from a person's heart: evil thoughts, sexual immorality, theft, murder, adultery, greed, wickedness, deceit, lustful desires, envy, slander, pride and foolishness. Like a sandwich, He concludes this section with the same statement He began with, *"All these vile things come from within; they are what defile you"* (v. 23).

Jesus is making a distinct connection within the entire passage of Mark 7:1-23. While the Pharisees fumed over the disciples' unclean hands, Jesus shows them He is more concerned with unclean hearts. The ceremonial washing of their hands (and other items) was imposed and elevated above their concern for purifying their hearts. Ceremonially unclean hands don't defile us, only unclean hearts. Jesus reinforced this by teaching that even the foods we eat don't defile us, but rather what comes from within.

Heart Exam

5. From Mark 7:21-23, what unclean things have spilled out of you in the last week or month? Which of these do you struggle with the most? How do you guard yourself against these evils?

6. How have you been misguided into thinking that if you keep things in check externally, you are okay spiritually?

7. Are you more concerned with the things that enter your stomach or the things that enter your heart? Why? How would others know this about you?

God is more concerned with cleansing our hearts of corruption and purifying our spiritual pollution. The Pharisees missed the heart of the matter. While flagrant in their façade, the fault of the Pharisees was their fraudulent hearts. We would be wise to remember that man-made traditions will never be a substitute for inward cleanliness—nor will they have the power to purify us. We don't become good on the inside by doing the right things; rather, we do the right things because we are clean on the inside.

The condition of our hearts will always be the crux of our relationship with God. Who we really are is who we are on the inside, not who we portray on the outside. Thankfully, God is in the business of heart cleansing. When we surrender our hearts to His gracious love and His masterful touch, He will show us areas of weakness and begin to supernaturally cleanse us from within. The beauty of a pure heart will always be what God desires.

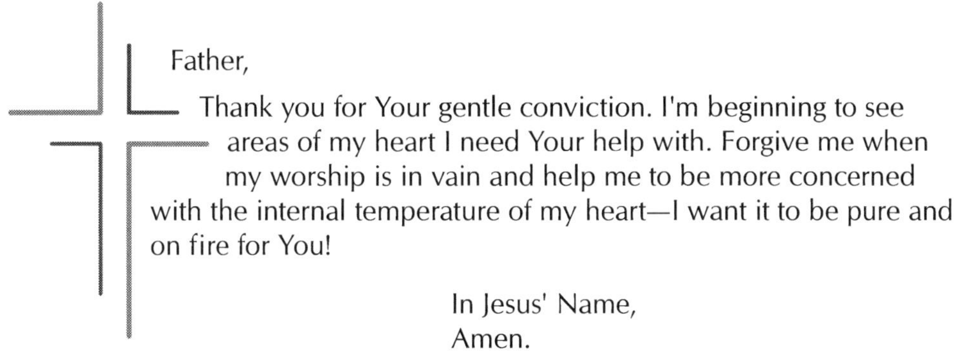

Father,

Thank you for Your gentle conviction. I'm beginning to see areas of my heart I need Your help with. Forgive me when my worship is in vain and help me to be more concerned with the internal temperature of my heart—I want it to be pure and on fire for You!

In Jesus' Name,
Amen.

Day 3: Bridging The Gap

Cleansing our hearts brings us to a place of maintaining clear consciences before God. When we become aware change is needed we seek the Changer to renovate us from within. Of course this isn't a one-time occurrence. Heart examination needs to remain on the forefront of our minds each day as we walk toward Christlikeness.

Read Matthew 23:25-28

Here we find Jesus again, addressing the internal wickedness of the Pharisees. He notes their meticulous nature to ensure that cups and dishes are sparkling on the outside, but remain filthy on the inside. He compares these people to whitewashed tombs, beautiful on the outside, but full of death within. The Law rendered anything connected to death as unclean. In today's terms, a mere visit to Grandma's grave would make us contaminated. Tombs in the first century were whitewashed, usually with lime or plaster, so they were obvious and easily avoided. [1] This served as a warning against defilement. The word for whitewashed is a *"term applied to a hypocrite who conceals his malice under an outward assumption of piety."* [2]

In true 'Jesus' fashion, He targets the one area, which though hidden to others, is not concealed from Him—the heart. His words puncture the Pharisees' puffed-up lives. The Messiah's accusations unnerve them. How dare this man gouge their flaunted gifts, lance their legalism, penetrate their pride and ruin their pious reputation.

The Pharisees can no longer hide their hypocrisy in the face of Christ. Jesus calls them blind. Their eyes fail to see the real spiritual filth pouring from their hearts. Jesus tells them what they should do: *"First wash the inside of the cup and dish, and then the outside will become clean, too"* (v. 26). Of course this is a play on words, as Jesus is referring to washing their hearts first. It's not their outsides that made them unclean, but their insides. He is teaching that we are to be more concerned with keeping our internal cup clean rather than showing a glowing external false pretense. Until we clean the inside—our hearts—we will lack the fruit of an honest life free from hypocrisy.

The result of cleaning our insides is that it will naturally affect our outsides. We'll never be pure externally if we're not pure within. All of our "righteous" acts will be considered rubbish if our hearts are soiled.

Heart Exam

It's time to do dishes friends! Like the Pharisees, we can no longer hide our hypocrisy in the face of Christ. Jesus says in Mark 23:26 we should *"First wash the inside of the cup."*

---

1 *The Adam Clarke Commentary. http://classic.studylight.org/com/acc/view.cgi?book=mt&chapter=23&verse=27#Mt23_27 (accessed: 2-5-2013).*

2 *http://classic.studylight.org/isb/bible.cgi?query=matthew+23%3A25-28§ion=0&it=nas&oq=mattew%252023%3A%252025-28&ot=bhs&nt=na&new=1 (accessed: 2-5-2013).*

Day 3

1. What needs washed in your heart? What steps are you willing to take to purge yourself of "self" and restore your heart to God today, this week, this month and this year?

2. What kind of exterior "things" do you do in an effort to camouflage your inner self? Do you recognize how these things are really a mask disguising your sin?

Many people focus on outward appearances while neglecting the most important aspect of their lives. There are many reasons for this, but one specifically is that it's easier to keep the outside clean. I mean, really, who wants others to see the real us, right? Isn't it less work to just go through the motions and not have to deal with our own disgust? We can wear the right clothes, makeup and jewelry, get the right haircut and drive the nice car. We can even have an opulent house and serve in children's ministry each week. Yet, no matter how 'right' our exteriors may appear, they will never equal a right heart.

Maybe we've grown so accustomed to acting the right way that we've become disconnected from The Way. Like the Pharisees and teachers of the Law, we can know the right stuff but it may never penetrate any further than our heads. Do we really know God, or do we merely know about God? Head knowledge is different from heart transformation. The purpose of biblical information **is** transformation. If biblical truth only enters our minds and never penetrates our hearts, our lives will increasingly resemble the Pharisees.

> When I was younger my life became void of a personal exchange with God. The information of God's Word was contained in my head but it didn't reach beyond my neck. My heart floundered and I began to drown in robotic rituals. I waded in stagnant waters of programmed prayers, manufactured worship and monotonous devotions while my heart shifted toward shallowness.
>
> I managed to reduce my relationship with God to a list. My spiritual inventory looked something like this: Let's get this done so I can get on with my day. Read the Bible for ten minutes. Check. Pray for five minutes. Check. Glance over this week's study. Check. Go to church. Check. Go to Bible study. Check.

Day 3

Maybe a similar list has swirled in your head. Each week you follow your religious agenda only to find yourself void of spiritual depth and companionship. In your quest to conquer your to-do list and 'earn points' with God, you go through the motions with no connection to your heart.

Heart Exam

3. How have you been guilty of a spiritual checklist? What does yours look like?

4. Do programmed prayers, manufactured worship and monotonous devotions describe the current state of your relationship with God? If not, how would you described it?

No matter how 'right' exteriors may appear, they will never equal a right heart.

Many of us know what we ought to do, but fail to have the "want-to." For example, we know we should read our Bibles and pray, but when we do, our hearts may not be engaged. We know we should go to church, but we're unmotivated. Maybe we view our time in the Word as homework or a chore that needs done. It's important to understand what motivates us spiritually. Spiritual maturity can sometimes be measured by the purity of our motives.

The real issue is bridging the eighteen-inch gap: the distance between the head and the heart. Knowing what we "ought-to" do and possessing the "want-to" are at opposite ends of the spectrum. The "want-to" of the heart must outweigh the "ought-to" of the head. Changing the motives of one's heart is more than mere head knowledge; it is heart penetration and transformation.

We may intuitively know in our minds the things of God, but knowing them is different from receiving them. When the things of God puncture our hearts we make the relationship our own and personally stake a claim to it. We are drawn to the arms of a loving God with passion and purpose—seeking Him is our utmost priority.

When we reduce our relationship with Christ to a list of rules and rituals we will fail to experience an intimate relationship with Him. Following "rules" doesn't make us Christians—but following Christ does! We need more than a change of behavior; we need a change of heart.

> Through heartbreaking tragedy, God radically altered my life. He brought to light profound weaknesses and gaping holes in my counterfeit Christianity. He shattered my perfectionism, He demolished my pride and He leveled my legalism. God taught me that my desire should be to love Him with all of my heart, not just pieces of it here and there.

Day 3

> The intimacy I now share with Christ is rich because He bridged the eighteen-inch gap in my life. My purpose for doing the same things I did before, now stems from an undivided love for my Savior. He replaces complacency with a passionate pursuit of Him. He sets me free from being a "good" Christian to being a devoted follower.
>
> Please hear my heart: I don't perfectly love God. Yes, He restored my life, but I still must guard my heart from plastic prayers, superficial service and wooden worship. There are days I am tempted to go through the motions, but I must remind myself I am created for more. Why would I trade genuine intimacy with God for counterfeit closeness? When I do go through "the motions," I fail to experience a deeper relationship with God.

Our "want-to" stems from the expanse of our love, recognition of our desperate need for Christ and the Holy Spirit, while remembering what it means to be touched by grace. The more we love, the more we desire to please our Lord. The more we love, the more we sacrifice to strengthen this relationship. The more we love, the more we do things from a pure heart, not from seeking our own glory or crown.

The motive behind each choice makes all the difference with the spiritual temperature of one's inner being. God knows our intentions. We must purge our tendency to look good externally. Instead, we must strive to make our hearts right, which in turn will produce a heart with pure intentions. A pure heart strives for internal purity not merely external piety.

Our motives change when we are challenged to do things as a result of what Christ has done for us. The natural overflow of one's heart is the love of Christ that we cannot contain and are compelled to share. This love penetrates the poison in our hearts and motivates us to live genuine Christian lives. This transformation enables us to live a life beyond hypocrisy.

A heart rightly aligned with Christ loves God and His Word out of devotion not duty; out of love, not a list; out of a relationship, not rules and rituals. 1 Chronicles 28:9b reminds us to *"Serve God with wholehearted devotion and with a willing mind, for the Lord searches every heart and understands every motive behind the thoughts."*

♡ ***Heart Exam***

5. Share the ways eighteen inches affects you. How well do you understand that head knowledge about God is not enough?

6. What situations contribute to reducing your relationship with God to a list?

Day 3

7. What is your motivation for living the Christian life? How can the "want-to" of your Christian walk be revived?

Cleansing the inside enables the heart to connect to the head. Like the Pharisees, we often know how to talk, act, and live the Christian life (or what we think it is), but we fail to connect the eighteen-inch gap between the head and the heart. When the heart is purified, this distance isn't so distant. Head knowledge can then penetrate our core and result in heart transformation.

DAY 4: Resumé Righteousness

Lack of internal cleansing negates pure external actions. As Christians, it is vital to understand why we do what we do. Our passion, our purpose and our mission to the furtherance of the gospel echoes the depth of our motives and purity of heart. In today's study we're going to dig even deeper. This may be a hard lesson for some, but let's stay the course and be open to what God may want to teach us.

In the American culture that praises performance, we are hard pressed to possess pure intentions. In addition, much of what we do can be driven by the "I can somehow 'earn' God's favor" vehicle. This thinking stems from the enemy's pursuit to convince us we actually have something to do with salvation and its maintenance. We can't earn salvation or save ourselves. God offers salvation and we can't receive it without a response of faith. If the enemy can trip up our thoughts and motives in this area, we corner ourselves in the performance cage.

Our beloved brother, apostle Paul, who was a respected Pharisee, clearly shows us how confidence in our flesh inhibits our intimacy and worship of God. For today, we'll take a look at Paul's life and his recommendation for those who seek to put hope and righteousness in human accomplishments. We'll also witness his fierce warning to the Philippians to be on guard against those teaching evil, which Paul concluded, were those who were enforcing confidence in the flesh.

Read Philippians 3:3-9

If anyone had a stellar resumé, it was Paul. He was the Jewish epitome of "having it all." To accurately understand why his resumé was so extraordinary we must view Scripture through a first-century lens. Verse 5 starts with an entourage of items Paul could have taken confidence in.

Let's take a closer look at the seven things Paul reveals about his heritage and righteousness that he could have boasted in. Devout Jews adhered to Old Testament Law and circumcised males on the eighth day after birth. Paul's parents made sure their obedience to the Law was carried out. Paul was born into Judaism; he wasn't converted later in life. Being of the people of Israel is significant because they were God's chosen people. Paul was from the original vine; he wasn't grafted in later. Being from the tribe of Benjamin also carried weight as it was viewed as one of the leading tribes of the twelve. As a Hebrew of Hebrews, Paul was at the top of the elite in keeping his Jewish heritage. In regards to the Law, being a Pharisee elevated a person to higher stature, revealed a deep understanding of the Scriptures and expectations for right living. Paul's zeal for persecuting the church was praised by his peers who did the same. He was intent not to let this infectious disease, regarding a man named Christ, spread throughout any region. Paul's legalistic righteousness was faultless because he abided by the strictest guidelines of Judaism and, most likely, many man-made traditions.

Day 4

At first glance we may not think Paul's resumé looks anything like ours: we're not Jewish and we're certainly not from the same family line or nation. Regardless, there is some powerful take away for us in this passage.

♡ Heart Exam

1. What Christian heritage and personal righteousness could you wrongly take confidence in? Be specific.

Perhaps we unknowingly take stock in our Christian lineage. For example, "*I was born and raised in the church. I've been a Christian my whole life. I was dedicated as a baby and confirmed in junior high. Great Grandpa Henry served in this church; the seventh pew from the front has his named etched on it. And, my Aunt Lucy led the choir for twenty years.*" Or, "*Well, my family name and our service to the church has been known in this community for years.*"

Or maybe, we take too much pride in what denomination we identify with: "*I'm Catholic, Presbyterian, Episcopalian, Lutheran, Free Methodist, Baptist, Assembly of God, Reformed and Christian etc.*" When we identify with our denomination more than we identify ourselves as followers of Jesus Christ, we place false confidence in the flesh.

How about making sure others know what we do and don't do? Similar to the Pharisees who wanted to be noticed for all their righteous acts, do we seek to have others see what we do and don't do? Sometimes Christians are known for what they stand against more than what they stand for. "*Look at those tattoos and piercings. Can you believe she just put out a cigarette before walking into church? Doesn't he know he smells like alcohol?*" Or, let's make it more personal, "*I would never watch R-rated movies. I would never gamble or even walk into a casino. Our children do not play sports on the Sabbath. We tithe 15%, not just 10%. I don't drive above the speed limit. Homeschooling is the only way to educate children.*"

> *"Or there's 'reverse confidence in the flesh:' Some Christians may boast in their freedom and look down on those uptight religious types. So they feel smug about their freedom to show off tattoos or the edgy-ness of their church or their freedom to drink beer, wine, or what-have-you. Either way they're boasting in themselves rather than in Christ."* [1]

1 *Quote by Dr. John Whittaker, Professor of Preaching & New Testament, Boise Bible College, Boise, Idaho. June 28, 2013.*

Day 4

2. Based on the previous paragraph and quote, what thoughts would you add that you have quietly uttered to yourself or that you secretly think? Be honest, we all have them. Acknowledging them helps us to remove them. After you write your items, ask God to help you rearrange your thoughts when these judgments and/or self-exaltations present themselves.

Before we assume we don't persecute the church we would be wise to evaluate how we view other denominations. Perhaps we don't agree with their doctrine or what they practice and because of it we won't even associate with others from "that" church. Or, when we're introduced to someone new and they share what church they attend, we immediately check them off of our friend list. It's okay to disagree over non-essentials, but we cannot forget The Church is beyond the walls of where we attend each week. Our particular church or denomination is also not the only one that will be in heaven. Regardless of label, followers of Christ Jesus will join around the throne of God together, as one.

Hopefully, we are beginning to understand how we can unintentionally take great confidence in our flesh. Who we are, our family name, denominational label or what we do and don't do can all impact our tendency to boast in ourselves.

Now, re-read your items in question 1, then add any more that have come to mind.

Let's go back to the first part of this passage in Philippians to grasp this issue full circle. Please re-read Philippians 3:3-9. Remember, Paul is warning his audience to watch out for "dogs and mutilators of the flesh" (v. 2). Paul is referring to those who are part of the false circumcision and are spreading this false teaching. After Paul accepted Christ, he often fought an uphill battle with Judiazers who infiltrated the churches. They taught that a Gentile (non-Jew) must first become a Jew in order to be saved. This meant an individual would be required to be circumcised before becoming a Christian. Circumcision was an external physical mark showing their membership into the nation of Israel, God's chosen people. One could not be considered a Jew without this operation.

Circumcision was part of the Old Testament Law, but Christ's sacrifice nullified this teaching as necessary. Paul declares, "No!" Circumcision is not required for a person to be saved. The Judaizers however, continued to adhere to this faulty belief of the essentialness of circumcision. Their confidence was placed in this physical brand on the body rather than on Christ's work on the cross. Paul also teaches in Romans 2:28-29, true circumcision is of the heart. He also reiterates in Galatians 5:6 that *"In Christ Jesus neither circumcision nor uncircumcision has any value."* Paul emphatically teaches the only way to escape God's wrath is for Jew and Gentile alike to accept the atoning death of Christ.

Romans 2:28-29

28 A man is not a Jew if he is only one outwardly, nor is circumcision merely outward and physical. 29 No, a man is a Jew if he is one inwardly; and circumcision is circumcision of the heart, by the Spirit, not by the written code. Such a man's praise is not from men, but from God.

Day 4

Paul is not suggesting that his Jewish upbringing, the Law and the rest of his resumé are wicked, but the attitude to place confidence in them is. When Paul converted to Christianity he had to relinquish the notion that he and God somehow worked together for his justification. Instead, he had to realign his beliefs to accept that his righteousness and justification came by God's provision through Christ. Paul gains Christ because of his willingness to consider himself acquitted based purely on Jesus' death. [2]

In this section of Scripture Paul rejects the Judaizers' requirements and additions to the gospel of grace. Paul instructs that we cannot trust in the flesh AND submit to the gospel; this is contradictory. When we surrender to the gospel it reveals our absolute faith in Christ's atoning blood and not our resumé of righteousness.

> The only way I knew to be liked or loved growing up was to excel at EVERYTHING and be known as the "good girl" . . . and this I did.
>
> I failed to comprehend a love greater than: 110lbs., 4.0 GPA, All-League Softball, National Honor Society, ASB President . . . blah, blah, blah! It was all an external cover-up for an internal fall-out. Grace was a girl's name, not the condition of my Christian life and salvation.
>
> Living with performance shackles negatively influenced my walk with God. I put stock in my resumé of righteousness, keeping a mental tally of why "Hester is an A+ Christian." This bondage pushed me to try and prove myself to God. I whipped out my resumé of qualifications to convince Him why He should love me or want me. I kept people at arm's length so they could never see my heart. My view of others was also skewed because of the corrupt lens I looked through.

As mentioned on Day 3, a series of events pummeled me to my knees before God. And . . . I fell hard. I began to accurately see myself and others in view of who God is. In time God tenderly removed the seed of perfection and replaced it with the salve of His grace. Accepting and truly living in His love reduced my resumé to ashes. Every broken piece of my unfulfilled heart bears the scars of divine intervention.

Our culture praises performance. Schools and colleges grade assignments accordingly. Athletics and the Arts celebrate advancements. Corporate accomplishments elevate pay, position and power, with another notch to add to the resumé. Rewards motivate. Kudos fuel our nature to prove ourselves. It's not necessarily bad to want to do our best or improve. The problem comes when the performance mindset transfers into our relationship with God. There is no other place where performance doesn't pay off.

♡ *Heart Exam*

3. Do you accurately understand what it means to be saved by grace? Are you keeping score of your good works?

---

2 *NIV Application Commentary/Philippians by Frank Thielman, Zondervan Publishers @ 1995 pg 165-192.*

4. How are you tempted to prove your worth to God? How would perfection, performance and pleasing others affect your relationship with God?

5. What are symptoms of performance living? Which ones plague you? (Although there are many, here are a few to start with: Need to succeed, guilt and shame over the past, improper boundaries, appearing "put together," inability to say "no," etc.)

The core truth of Christianity is that we cannot **ever** earn our salvation. If we could somehow gain righteousness and/or salvation through our own "works" then Christ's death was not necessary. In Galatians 2:21 Paul exhorts, *"I do not set aside the grace of God, for if righteousness could be gained through the law, Christ died for nothing!"* It is by faith we receive the righteousness of God—through His sacrifice on the cross. The only "work" required of us: *"to believe in the One He has sent"* (John 6:29).

Resumé righteousness will never make us righteous, only Redeemer righteousness makes us righteous.

2 Corinthians 5:21 reminds us, *"God made him who had no sin to be sin for us, so that in him we might become the righteousness of God."*

Accepting Christ means we exchange:

† our filth for His forgiveness
† our garbage for His grace
† our refuse for His redemption
† our sin for His salvation
† our boasting for His blood

Day 4

Ephesians 2:8-9 clarifies we are saved by grace through faith. *"For it is by grace you have been saved, through faith—and this is not from yourselves, it is the gift of God—not by works, so that no one can boast."* Salvation has nothing to do with the works we have done or presently do. Otherwise, we might gloat over our virtue and wave our resumé of righteous living to show that we deserve approval.

This faulty thinking causes us to assume we can somehow earn God's favor. When we operate under this presupposition we fail to understand the depth of our depravity and need for Christ's sacrifice. This erroneous thinking also deludes our motivation for serving the Lord. What should be born out of gratitude and love results in duty-driven living compelled by obligation and score-keeping. When we focus on what we do and how good we think we are, we lose focus of the cross.

♡ ***Heart Exam***

6. C'mon, now it's your turn. What's your resumé look like? Make a detailed list of every significant accomplishment, job promotion, title, education, award or man-made rule that you follow, that you could mistakenly fall prey to gloat in. Feel free to write on another sheet of paper. Please don't skip this portion. It is an important part of today's lesson and you'll discover why later.

Like Paul, we may have many credentials and other achievements we could boast in. While we certainly cannot choose the heritage we were brought up in, many of our accolades may have come to us through human effort. These are not wrong unless we falsely put security in them as a way to prove our righteousness before God or elevate self above others. Efforts to win God's approval and refusal to embrace salvation by faith, denies an accurate understanding of the Gospel of Christ.

Day 4

Keeping an accurate perspective of why we do good things is vital. Ephesians 2:10 teaches we were created to do good things. However, we don't do them to get saved; we do them because we are saved! We come to Christ empty handed. He in turn fills us, so our hands can be used *for* **Him**—not for ourselves. Our motivation changes from performance-driven to Kingdom-driven.

Even though we live in an achievement-driven culture we must resist our tendency to validate ourselves to God and others. We live for a King and we seek the applause of One. Maintaining a constant awareness of our continual need for Christ's grace enables our hearts not to be elevated to a place of misplaced security. Praise God no resumé is needed with Him.

Heart Exam

7. What has impacted you the most from today's lesson? Spend extra time in prayer evaluating the present condition of where your confidence lies.

Ephesians 2:10

[10]For we are God's workmanship, created in Christ Jesus to do good works, which God prepared in advance for us to do.

During the inaugural teaching of this study a friend commented on her resumé:

"The resumé I once boasted of on paper to impress others means nothing to the One who means everything."

Sue Overland

Day 5: Uncover the Cover-up

Yesterday's lesson was longer than usual, but I hope our hearts are full as God continues to cleanse and refresh our internal and eternal perspectives. My prayer as we progress through this study is to spend the necessary time for self-examination to rightly align our hearts with Christ. We need this every day.

Our final day this week will again touch a sensitive nerve. Specifically, we'll address the positive and negative effects of living as authentic Christians. Whether we acknowledge it or not, how we live impacts everyone around us, whether for good or bad.

As mentioned in prior lessons we live in a world of exteriors. As we've quickly discovered, the Pharisees and teachers of the Law provide us with ample evidence. Covering up is sadly, second nature. Because so much in our lives is based on externals, we forget the importance of living genuinely and risking vulnerability for the sake of Kingdom building. Living real in a cover-up world does not come naturally.

When our lives are driven by performance, not only will we be unable to accurately live by God's grace, we will struggle to share His grace with others. This will be revealed by how much we strive to cover-up our faults for the sake of self-preservation. Being authentic is inhibited because we want others to think everything is "just fine." Sound familiar? I've been there too.

Recently I witnessed a lady share the testimony of her daughter overcoming great difficulty. Her story was touching and heartfelt. Towards the end she began to tear up and shield her face. Then, as her voice began to crackle, she said those two familiar words, "I'm sorry." She feared losing composure was inappropriate for her testimony. She truly had nothing to be sorry for, but isn't this like us to retract when we begin to reveal our true feelings. What will people think of me? Right?

Shortly before this instance, I witnessed a group of individuals at Celebrate Recovery. CR is a 12-step Christian program to assist people in overcoming their hurts, habits and hang-ups. My friend shared her testimony this night and I wanted to support her courage. After she finished, one by one, participants made their way to the microphone introducing themselves and the specific sin and struggle they faced. *"Hello my name is ___________, and I ___________."* Pornography, anorexia, bulimia, anger, alcohol, drugs, gluttony, prescription medication, control, perfectionism and sex were a few mentioned this night. You know, just fluff stuff with nothing too deep or personal. (I hope you hear the sarcasm.) Everyone was welcomed and I sensed not an ounce of condemnation, but rather hope. People were at different stages in their recovery and hearing others' victory brought encouragement to all.

Our tendency as Christians is to make sure outward appearances are in order and look good to others. Fears of what others might think of us are crippling aren't they? If we cannot be transparent Christians our intention will be to cover up what we don't want others to notice or pretend to be something we are not. Self-protection is our natural response. Human inclination wants others to perceive the best in us. We falsely think if the exterior is attractive, it will mask any ugliness of the interior. Consider the last class reunion you attended. Boy, if that isn't an event of masquerading I don't know what is.

Day 5

What if? What if we removed our masks of pretense, indifference and perfection? What if we allowed others to see the real us? It is necessary for those bearing the name of Christ not to pretend but let people observe us authentically. When we are genuine, we will be vulnerable enough to admit we don't have it all together and our desire will be to show others God's grace despite our personal weaknesses and flaws.

♡ Heart Exam

1. We are all tempted to hide our imperfections and struggles. Various fears cause us to cover-up, which inhibits authenticity. What stops you from sharing your weaknesses with others?

We may or may not have an addiction like the CR example I shared. But we all have sin, faults and real life flaws. Marital, parental and financial difficulties are some common examples. Fear of exposure prevents us from seeking help and being transparent enough to openly share our struggles. This is not about putting them on display, but for the purpose of accountability and expressing our hope in Christ to others. I'm not suggesting we empty our closet, but rather be real enough to offer encouragement to folks because we've "been there" or we are there. We all wrestle with various weaknesses. So why pretend we don't? Others must see how we cope.

We are not part of some perfect club and others are not invited. Truth is, we're part of the redeemed club and everyone is invited.

When we are genuine it makes us approachable and God relate-able to mankind. This is unlike the Pharisees and their practices of them we studied this week. When we admit our imperfections and show others we are a work in progress, it exhibits our utter dependence upon God and our need for Him to walk with us through life. If we had a "perfect" life we wouldn't need Jesus.

> *2 Corinthians 12:9*
>
> [9]*But he said to me, "My grace is sufficient for you, for my power is made perfect in weakness."* Therefore I will boast all the more gladly about my weaknesses, so that Christ's power may rest on me.

God often uses our scars and weaknesses to draw others to Him. Part of our testimony is bearing the wounds we endure in life. Because of Him, we are hopeful not hopeless. We can offer the hope of Christ because our faith is a living declaration of this hope. The power of the risen Christ dwells in us. We are, therefore, equally empowered to overcome whatever we wrestle.

Our openness also allows seekers to witness the radiance of Christ in us. The beauty revealed is the work He has completed and the work He continues to accomplish in us. Proving to the world that healing and victory are available in Christ delivers a correct estimation of who God is: Redeemer, Restorer and Life-giver. Hiding this glory steals an opportunity for others to behold His redemptive power.

In addition, authenticity also declares God's splendor by disclosing that His power is indeed made perfect in our weakness, as 2 Corinthians 12:9 claims. When we acknowledge our shortcomings, we put ourselves in a position to receive His strength. Then we can exalt His name by walking in triumph and credit our conquering life where credit is due.

Day 5

Heart Exam

2. When the opportunity presents itself do you shrink back in fear or do you boldly proclaim Christ's power in your life in order to give Him glory?

3. Different challenges come and go, but God's faithfulness to help us through them is always apparent. How are you specifically growing from your difficulties? How can you share your growth with others in order to extend the hope of Christ?

4. Your testimony is a powerful witness. How willing are you to share with others what God "has done" and "is doing" in and through your life? Also, share how you have been encouraged by another's testimony.

5. What are some positive and negative effects of living authentically as a Christian? How does this impact others?

Praise from men is a powerful deterrent for authentically proclaiming the gospel through our lives. We see this example in John 12:42-43. *"Yet at the same time many even among the leaders believed in him [Christ]. But because of the Pharisees they would not confess their faith for fear they would be put out of the synagogue; for they loved praise from men more than praise from God."* God needs to be really **BIG** and man needs to remain really **small** for the praise of men to be meaningless to us.

There are natural consequences for our belief in Jesus Christ. Some may be positive and others may be negative. When we allow fear of what they might be or what others may think, we welcome the approval of man over the approval of God. Accepting man's praise is another way of pursuing external piety, which ultimately inhibits the gospel message in our lives. Pursuing internal purity authentically promotes the evidence of the gospel message through our lives.

Day 5

Heart Exam

6. What do you want others to see in you? What may need to be uncovered?

7. Praise from people can promote external piety in our lives. What praise from men could become a stumbling block to you?

8. How are you prohibiting or promoting the gospel message in your life? How obvious is Christ's power in you?

Remember from yesterday's lesson, our desire to appear righteous to others is a faulty view that we can somehow climb our way up a spiritual ladder. Recognizing our position in Christ keeps us humble because we acknowledge there is absolutely nothing we can "do" to look good or gain His saving favor.

At first glance it may not appear this passage connects to this study. However, the point Paul makes in this passage is the very thing the Pharisees rejected. They resisted the truth, yet continued in their false ways. Their demise will also be ours if we don't embrace and reflect this core truth in our relationship with Christ.

The central truth Paul is teaching the Corinthians is the glory of the new covenant in Christ. He contrasts the New and the Old by using a veil as a metaphor. His audience would have known the Old Testament Scriptures and been able to understand his point. He was trying to adequately show them that the glory of the Old Covenant pales in comparison to the New. (If needed, glance over Week One notes.)

The ministry of the new covenant is much greater and more glorious because we now walk according to the Spirit and His grace, not the Law. Paul is saying that one ministry brought death through the letter of the Law that was fading away. But the ministry of the new covenant comes through the Spirit Who gives life, and will not fade. The Israelites were frightened and didn't want to look upon the glory of the Lord so Moses covered his face with a veil (Exodus 34:29-35).

Day 5

9. Why do we cover our faces from others, yet be completely exposed to our Maker?

Even today, people's hearts are covered with a veil. They resist the glory of the Lord that is in Christ and the new covenant. But, for those who recognize Christ and accept His new covenant, the veil is removed and they are able to see the glory of the Lord. With unveiled faces, those who accept Christ reflect the glory of the Lord as they are transformed into His likeness.

We can have the same confidence, assurance, hope and boldness as Moses because we are of the new covenant. Our hope and boldness comes from this covenant and its lasting glory—through the blood of Christ, apart from the Law.

As we've learned, the Pharisees were guilty of covering up and being genuinely hypocritical. Their hearts were veiled to the Gospel of Christ. This passage in 2 Corinthians reminds us the veil conceals our hearts until we accept Christ. The very truth the Pharisees rejected was the glory of the new covenant. When we embrace the glory of the new covenant, we unveil our hearts and allow Christ's glory to be seen in us as we reflect Him to a perishing world.

Heart Exam

10. Maybe you've accepted Christ as your Lord and Savior but have never comprehended the glory of this covenant being revealed in your life. How adequately have you embraced the glory of the new covenant? Please share.

This glory has no pretense or pretending because it's not ours, but belongs solely to the Lord. When our purpose is to exude His glory, fear and inhibition melt as hypocrisy is chiseled away and authenticity is esteemed. We ultimately recognize our lives are all about Jesus Christ and furthering His kingdom. We can walk unashamed towards the Son knowing our life's plan is fulfilled in Him.

It's time to uncover the cover-up. Let's remove the inclination to hide pain and imperfections. May we stop pretending and start contending for what we profess. Replace shame and insecurity with Spirit empowered living and allow others a glimpse into the glorious work of Christ in our lives. This is authentic Christianity: living real in a cover-up world. Then we can repel our tendency to be fake, and instead, embrace living Christlike in a counterfeit culture.

VIEWER GUIDE

Philippians 3:3-9; 1 Samuel 16:7; Deuteronomy 6:5; Psalm 86:11;
1 Chronicles 28:9; Jeremiah 29:13

While the externals may look and feel right, we may neglect what matters most, the internal; ______ __________ .

How we identify ourselves can be found in where our _______________ _______ . Confidence in the cross, identifies ourselves in __________ . Confidence in the flesh, identifies ourselves in what _____ _____, instead of what's been _______ through Christ's death!

We mix-up our identity in the positions and titles we hold. This inhibits how we live out the roles we are in because we are always looking to ___________ ourselves in what _____ _____ .

Results:

1. Approval of ______.
2. Motivation to please _________ ________ , instead of God.
3. Externals become more important than the ____________.

Philippians 3:3-9 – Like Paul, we need to be willing to ________ the things of the flesh we would like to take confidence in; confidence in the ________ , not confidence in the flesh.

God has always been after our _________ .

1 Samuel 16:7 - God identifies us by what is on the __________ , while the world tries to identify us by what is on the ____________ .

"Love the Lord your God with all your heart." He doesn't want ________ of it – He __________ _____ of it! When God has our hearts . . . He has __________________ !

This internal heart ___________________________, will naturally affect our external life ____________________ .

Only Christ and the unadulterated Gospel provide the unwavering strength an established life well-built on Him yields, where our confidence and identity lie in the _________ ___ ________ , _____ _________________ .

1. What we do will be funneled through the truth that we are identified in Christ and what He has done.
2. It is going to matter who God says we are, not the culture we live in.
3. Our insecurities will find security in Christ.
4. The choices we make will be a response of faith, not fear.
5. We won't strive for man's approval because the opinions of others will depreciate.
6. Our motivation will change from glory of self to glory of God.

WEEK THREE

The Unbalanced See-Saw

Day 1

A Law Keeper's Demise

Day 2

Judge Who? - part 1

Day 3

Judge Who? - part 2

Day 4

Free To Live

Day 5

Unity of Grace & Truth

WEEK THREE—THE UNBALANCED SEE-SAW

Day 1: A Law Keeper's Demise

As we shift into week three my hope is that we will digest what we've learned so far. Each week's lessons build on the next. Last week we evaluated our hearts. We discussed the heart's motives and the necessity to embrace internal purity over external piety. In a world of performance-based living, it is vital we grasp this truth. Without constantly guarding why we do what we do, we reduce our spiritual growth to routine, comfort and knowledge. This external piety inhibits authentic intimacy with Christ.

The topic for this week will stretch and challenge us even more. Based on the heart work accomplished last week, we will begin to see how the purity of our hearts presently impacts how we relate to God. Regardless of which side of the see-saw we presently sit on, this week's lessons may be a delicate issue for some. Many factors influence our current understanding of legalism and grace. Finding a biblical balance and accurate comprehension will only propel us into a more meaningful relationship with God.

One side of the see-saw exhibits strictness with no room for error. Life is lived in a uniform box without any relinquishment of control. This law-keeper is often critical and harsh toward self and others. He/she struggles to be open-minded towards new ideas and tends to shy away from bold steps of faith. A legalist like this fails to understand God's grace and neglects to embrace Christ's sacrifice for what it's really worth.

The other side of the see-saw is what my husband calls pre-meditated grace. *"I know what God says, but I'll ask for His forgiveness later."* This person drinks grace like it's free and then gets in line for another refill when they're faced with a sinful choice. They live without considering their example or consequences to the name of Christ. They live oblivious to the truth that God's grace is a gift that cost Christ His very life. If this is our tendency, then we too fail to accurately understand God's grace and, to our demise, we inaccurately represent the gospel.

1. What is the quandary with legalism and the dilemma with pre-meditated grace? Why is biblical balance necessary?

Day 1

2. Based on the previous descriptions, mark below where you presently sit on this see-saw.

There is a lot of middle ground between these two. Within each position are symptoms and consequences we will address this week based on what we glean from the Word of God and the life of the Pharisees and teachers of the Law.

Read Luke 10:25-37

Don't lose sight of deeper truths within the familiarity of the parable of the Good Samaritan. Legalism seeks to justify self. Remember, this man was an expert in the Law. He had the necessary information and he accurately communicated what the Law required. He got a 100% for answering correctly. He knew what he was doing when he tested Christ; however, he failed to anticipate Jesus' response.

As an expert in the Law, he would have known the duty of a priest and Levite to aid this poor man's needs. But never would he expect Christ to use a Samaritan to rescue him. Samaritans were the unwanted and unlovely race at the bottom of the social ladder. It was culturally unacceptable for a Samaritan to assist a Jew, yet this was who Christ used to be the hero of the story. It was no accident. Christ knew the expert in the law only wanted to justify himself. Christ turned the tables on his legalism to show the man that while he may be able to know and obey the right laws, he neglected more important matters of the heart. The mercy ship went to sea without him. In essence, Jesus is asking the lawyer, *"Will you be this kind of neighbor, regardless of convenience, prejudice, schedule and money?"*

Heart Exam

3. How do you seek to justify yourself before God? Do you see any similarities in your life compared to the lawyer; having the right information, but lacking application?

Day 1

4. It might be time for an attitude check on our perspective. Do you tend to keep all the right rules, but fail to extend mercy where needed? Or, perhaps neglect to see a deeper need within a situation?

Will you be this kind of neighbor, regardless of convenience, prejudice, schedule and money?

5. How do convenience, prejudice, money and schedules get in the way of ministering to the needs of others? What kind of neighbor are you really?

Legalism can creep its way into our lives when we neglect to remember that we cannot ever justify ourselves; only the blood of Christ can justify our sinfulness. Law keepers are prone to take pride in what they do and don't do, trying to appear holy in the eyes of others. They can also slide into works based righteousness.

Let's look at another aspect of legalistic living. Legalistic people are also very quick to expose the faults of others, but never themselves. Remember self-preservation? This kicks in when we want to reveal the sins of others. We think if everyone is looking at them, then they certainly won't be looking at us. This mindset starts early on. Think of children and their tendency to point out their sibling's sin. *"Mommy, look at Johnny. He's eating all the cookies on the counter."* Interestingly, when mommy investigates Johnny, he points at his tattle-tale brother (whose face is smeared with chocolate no less) and says, *"Tommy told me to."*

Human nature will divert any attempt to call self out. The above example may arouse a chuckle, but even adults do this; you know, the people who should know better for goodness sake! The irony is that while we may certainly disclose others' weaknesses, we are equally wrong in the matter because we want others to think we don't have any flaws ourselves. Ugh! I am guilty as charged.

Read Luke 16:13-16

Jesus was teaching a parable to His disciples. He wraps up the point of His instruction from prior verses, in verse 13. Within ear shot are the scorning Pharisees who cannot stand the nerve of Christ to pin them to the bull's eye of a dart board. Jesus "has a way" of speaking directly to their sin doesn't He? They aren't too happy because Christ is insinuating money is an idol to them.

Then Jesus delivers heart-piercing truth, ***"You are the ones who justify yourselves in the eyes of men, but God knows your hearts. What is highly valued among men is detestable in God's sight."*** They are the ones who seek to appear righteous in the presence of men, but are unrighteous in the sight of God, because He's well acquainted with their interior makeup and motives.

Day 1

The things that are valued and exalted in our world should not be the things we strive for as Believers. Appearing righteous and worshiping money are two specifics addressed here. But, anything man exalts for himself cannot bring God glory. "Anything" could literally become a misplaced idol. In order to properly extol God and render the glory due His name, we must resist seeking any human accomplishment for the sake of self. When we seek to elevate self we position ourselves against God because He doesn't share His throne with anyone or anything.

♡ Heart Exam

6. As Jesus claims, God does know our hearts. What would He say is highly valued in your sight? Ask the Lord to show you if any of these are exalted above Him to a place of idol worship. If they're presently not, how could they become a snare to you?

7. How do you resist human accomplishment for the sake of self? What may need to change for your pursuits to be Kingdom-driven versus self-driven?

8. What kinds of things does our world exalt that Christians should try to steer clear of?

As we've learned today, legalism seeks to justify self and expose the faults of others—but never themselves. Staying balanced on the see-saw requires us to resist legalistic tendencies and not abuse the grace of God. This will help us repel the urge to justify ourselves and reveal the shortcomings of others.

Day 2: Judge Who? – part 1

Much criticism and controversy surround the topic for today's material. This lesson is one I've agonized over since the Lord gave me the outline for this study. Many prayers have been uttered for receptive hearts of those who read these words. I have no intent to be divisive but do believe this issue is one that needs to be courageously addressed despite resistance.

Judgment is a highly misunderstood topic; many reasons stem from the American culture of tolerance and mind-your-own-business. Many Christians are quick to say, *"That's judgmental! You're not the judge! God's the judge,"* without accurately comprehending Scripture and the responsibility fellow brothers and sisters in Christ share. First, let's understand there is a difference between being judgmental and making a judgment.

People make judgments without being judgmental. Judges score gymnasts according to their judgment of an athlete's performance. Our governing law has judges who make judgments based on evidence. Banks make judgments for home loan qualification based on consumer debt and credit score. Many judgments can be made without being judgmental.

For example, I can observe that my neighbor is 6' 2", is an avid hunter and likes reality television. I'm not judging his activity but stating what I can witness. This may seem trite, but the real mess comes when we make judgments about people's personal lives. A lady tells me all the woes in her marriage and how horrible her husband treats her, expecting complete sympathy. But when I start to probe and inquire of deeper personal things in her life—lack of respecting her husband faces her like a fastball. She then retorts, *"You can't say I'm disrespectful to my husband; that's judgmental!"* I wasn't judging her treatment of her husband; I was making an assessment based on factual information. If I were judgmental towards her I would have said, *"I can't believe you treat your husband like a dog. What kind of Christian are you? I would never do that to my man."* Being judgmental is an attitude of the heart seeking to prove someone wrong or elevate self above another individual.

Being judgmental is an attitude of the heart.

Since the Garden, when sin entered the world, our human response is to hide our sins from God and others (see Genesis 3:1-13). The nature of sin is darkness. Bringing truth into darkness is resisted because we don't want what is hidden to come to light. We do not like being held accountable for our sin. This lack of owning up and taking responsibility is the painstaking truth and is growing like a poison throughout Christianity.

Additionally, we fall prey to the cultural expectation of tolerance. Let's be clear, God does not tolerate sin. Liberal concessions are made under the guise of *"God accepts us just as we are."* Oh, true indeed, He does receive us right where we are. He's the only One able to get rid of our filth. Understanding who God is acknowledges He loves us enough not to leave us like we are. He didn't save us so we would sit and stew in our sins. He rescued us so we would reflect Him.

The other inaccurate fallacy circulating is the assumption our sins are private and do not impact those around us. This is foolish. Every choice we make affects others—whether good or bad. We need to look no further than Scripture to understand how our sins are not private and do in fact impact others. Achan's sin collided with his entire family and the nation of Israel fell

Day 2

by the sword over one man's choice (see Joshua 6:17-19; 7:1-26). Verse 11 in Joshua 7 reveals *"Israel has sinned; they . . . ."* Even though Achan was the culprit, the entire nation suffered the consequences of one man's poor decision.

Jonah is another example (see Jonah 1:1-17). Verse 12 reveals how his initial attempt to hide from God impacted the entire crew aboard the vessel heading for Tarshish. *"It is my fault that this great storm has come upon you."* God asked Jonah to preach against the sin of Nineveh—to confront their rebellion head on. He ran. God pursued. Jonah finally repented and relinquished, resulting in the entire city of Nineveh receiving God's truth and turning from their evil ways.

In the New Testament many of Paul's letters blatantly address sin in churches. His prayer is for believers to handle it properly and not malign the Word of God.

♡ *Heart Exam*

1. How do your choices affect others (spouse, children, family, friends, co-workers etc.)? Be very specific and cite examples.

2. What visible consequences of sin have you experienced? How has this impacted your family, friends, co-workers, neighbors or your children?

3. How does hiding our sin hurt not only ourselves, but God and the body of Christ?

4. God desires our sin to come to light. How does living in darkness inhibit us, our relationship with God and others?

Day 2

This is not a call to flash a neon light on every sin. The harsh reality is, we repel dealing with our sin. The pendulum has swung so far to the left that many churches don't even administer biblical church discipline anymore. We've become hyper-sensitive to facing sin. A blind eye is batted and rebellion is openly tolerated amongst Christians. James 5:16 exhorts us to confess our sins to each other. The principles of Matthew 18:15-17 are forgotten and what God declares as our responsibility is now labeled "judgmental." When Matthew 18 is properly administered most people pack up their Bibles, bulletins and bruised egos and move on to Ignore My Sin Church on the corner of Tolerant & Easy Street, hoping their sin isn't exposed there.

> *James 5:16*
>
> *[16]Therefore confess your sins to each other and pray for each other so that you may be healed. The prayer of a righteous man is powerful and effective.*

Hear me out; I'm speaking to those who've accepted Christ as Lord. We have no place to judge or expect non-Christians to live a godly life because their standards are not God's. Our responsibility is to lovingly show non-believers Christ's love and redemption. Beware however, because this light exposes the darkness. The contrast of what is not in a person's life may cause them to feel judged because their deeds are revealed, even though a person walking in the light is not judging them. Some people avoid the light because they know they are pursuing darkness. Eventually, those in darkness will be judged because the Light has come (John 3:16-21).

However, for those in Christ, God designed biblical standards for handling sin. *"Brothers, if someone is caught in a sin, you who are spiritual should restore him gently. But watch yourselves, or you also may be tempted"* (Galatians 6:1). When sin needs to be addressed, Scripture is clear that it is to be done by a mature person and for the sole purpose of restoring the individual. Remember, restoration is the goal, not condemnation.

Read 2 Corinthians 2:5-11

This account reveals someone in the Corinthian church needing to be rebuked. Paul urges the believers to reaffirm their love for him. When people are restored, the fruit of righteousness results in both parties. Biblical correction should not be harsh, resentful or judgmental. A spiritually mature person recognizes their weight of responsibility to address sin, but can also humbly admit they are not exempt from temptation themselves. The joy of restoration produces spiritual growth and peace within relationships in the body of Christ *and* becomes a defeat to the enemy.

2 Timothy 3:16-17, reminds us of four ways the Bible is useful. *"All Scripture is God-breathed and is useful for teaching, rebuking, correcting and training in righteousness, so that the man of God may be thoroughly equipped for every good work."* The Word of God properly equips us through instruction, reproof, correction and training in righteousness. This all-inclusive four-pack works together, which enables us to effectively minister to others and remain spiritually prepared. As much as we might like to dismiss or hide our offenses, part of teaching and training includes rebuke and correction.

Day 2

5. Share a time when you were confronted with your sin? How was it handled?

6. Share a time when you confronted another's sin. How were you received? Did you handle the situation delicately, with love and the right heart?

Is there someone God has brought to your mind during today's lesson with whom you may need to have a heart-to-heart talk about apparent sin in their life? Ask God to show you the best way to approach the situation with truth and love, seasoned with grace.

People confuse biblical correction, rebuke and restoration with being judgmental. Even handling minor conflict between people is sadly, resisted. People push others away to force them to mind their own business. Such turmoil arises when those confronted feel attacked, make faulty assumptions, become defensive and then are unwilling to repent.

Day 3: Judge Who? – part 2

Hopefully we are learning to discern the difference between making a judgment and being judgmental. The flip side to be addressed is the Pharisaical judgmental heart. The Pharisees certainly had no problem pointing out the sin of others. Their strict adherence to the letter of the Law encouraged quick criticism and condemnation. Without condoning sin, Christ approached such matters with correction and consoling. They were harsh and unmerciful, while Jesus shepherded sinful hearts with His grace.

The Pharisees' demeanor and lack of love in how they handled such instances immensely irritated Jesus. He was also angry because they failed to see their own sin. We know this attitude irritated Christ because he continually rebuked their judgmental pursuits.

An attitude of judgment can take root when we compare our lives with others. This was the Pharisees' demise. Because they were governed by the Law and even followed extra, unnecessary laws they enforced, they would easily target minute infractions or supposed transgressions. Remember, they strived for righteousness coming from works. When they looked around and saw others neglect what they embraced or those who obviously sinned, they were ready to flog every felon.

But Christ warns them countless times and tells them they are the ones in the wrong. Whenever we compare our lives to others' it's easy to look good because people will always fail to live completely upright and holy lives. Until we compare ourselves to Christ we inaccurately gauge our worthiness. True calculation reveals that we will always fall short. But by God's abundant grace, we can rise above our stigma of sin and accurately view ourselves according to Who Christ is and whom He teaches us to become—like Him, NOT them. We become like Him in death to self, in righteousness, in giving, in serving and in loving when we loosen our judgmental chains and regard everyone equally. An equalized comparison reveals we are all equally sinners, equally in desperate need of God's proportionate grace and impartial mercy.

An equalized comparison reveals we are all equally sinners, equally in desperate need of God's proportionate grace and impartial mercy.

♡ *Heart Exam*

1. We all have the tendency to compare our sin to someone else's. Or maybe we hear of some horrible atrocity and tell ourselves, *"Boy, I'm sure glad I'm not like them."* Does this really justify us spiritually? Why is sin comparison a poor gauge for our righteousness?

Day 3

2. How tempted are you to judge others who don't do the spiritual kinds of things you do? Are these additions to God's standards or perhaps personal convictions?

Read John 8:1-11

This passage of Scripture has been a favorite of mine for years. The tenderness of Christ is evident. His response to an attempt to trap Him is met with love for a sinful woman. I've always wondered, where's the man involved here? Adultery takes two.

By my front door I have a large painted rock with these words: *"He who is without sin, cast the first stone"* (John 8:7). This visible reminder helps me remember that my sin is much bigger than this boulder. It's also my way of welcoming everyone into our home with open arms rather than firearms. **No sin is too big for Jesus.**

Our antagonists can't wait to see what Jesus will do with this woman. C'mon Jesus, the Law says she is to be stoned. We can't fault the Pharisees for not knowing the Law. They knew what was right more than they knew their wrongs. Instead of slaying the sinner, Jesus stoops. Instead of pointing at her face, He used His finger to scribble in the dirt. Instead of humiliating her before the crowd, He brought home a lesson that penetrated their hearts. The convicted accusers left, but the Teacher lingered. His reproach: *I do not judge you worthy of punishment, but insist from now on, that you do not violate God's law.*

Heart Exam

Identify yourself in this passage:

- Are you the woman living in sin?
- Are you a Pharisee ready to pounce?
- Perhaps you're one of the onlookers wondering what will happen and what will be said?
- Or, are you like Christ, ushering in the unexpected charitable response?

3. When was the last time you were in a situation where a person should have been stuck up for instead of struck down? If you did not come to their aid, what prevented you from doing so?

Day 3

The story of the woman caught in adultery takes us to a passage in Matthew 7, where Jesus specifically addresses judging others.

Read Matthew 7:1-5 (Cross reference Luke 6:37-42)

Maybe you've experienced a similar incident like me. A recent evening at home proved to be a real doozy between our three boys. No one wanted to take responsibility; but everyone had someone to blame for everything that no one did. Sound familiar? These famous words are forever etched in my brain, "*Well . . . but my brother, he . . . uh . . . I didn't do it.*"

Our human nature likes to point a finger at others to show what we're not doing in order to justify ourselves. It seems easier to pick out the flaws, weaknesses and shortcomings in those around us. In an attempt to bolster our own egos we think if we're "not as bad as them" then we're not so bad, right?

Wrong!

Jesus' warnings in these passages are direct and two-fold. First, He teaches that we will receive the same judgment and mercy from God as we extend to others. Secondly, He exhorts us to not gaze at the splinter in our brother's eye without seeing and removing the telephone utility pole in our own. Jesus isn't saying we can't point out the speck in our brother's eye. He **is** teaching we can't even consider assisting them in the removal of their speck until the removal of our log.

> *Luke 6:37-42*
>
> [37]*Do not judge, and you*
> *will not be judged. Do not*
> *condemn, and you will not*
> *be condemned. Forgive,*
> *and you will be forgiven.*
> [38]*Give, and it will be given*
> *to you. A good measure,*
> *pressed down, shaken*
> *together and running over,*
> *will be poured into your lap.*
> *For with the measure you*
> *use, it will be measured to*
> *you.* [39]*He also told them*
> *this parable: Can a blind*
> *man lead a blind man? Will*
> *they not both fall into a pit?*
> [40]*A student is not above*
> *his teacher, but everyone*
> *who is fully trained will be*
> *like his teacher.* [41]*Why do*
> *you look at the speck of*
> *sawdust in your brother's*
> *eye and pay no attention to*
> *the plank in your own eye?*
> [42]*How can you say to your*
> *brother, Brother, let me take*
> *the speck out of your eye,*
> *when you yourself fail to*
> *see the plank in your own*
> *eye? You hypocrite, first*
> *take the plank out of your*
> *eye, and then you will see*
> *clearly to remove the speck*
> *from your brother's eye.*

Circle below which points may describe you:

- I want my husband to lead, but I won't submit.
- I want my children to listen to me, but I won't hear their hearts.
- I want the church to meet my needs, but I don't volunteer to help meet the needs within the body.
- I don't want others to gossip about me, but I have no problem sharing about others.
- I criticize other people's priorities and use of their time or money, yet I remain undisciplined myself.

4. What other examples of "logs" could you write for yourself?

____

____

____

____

Day 3

We must take away, dislodge and eliminate the very things seeking to give us permission to condemn others in order to justify ourselves. This external extraction first requires internal subtraction.

We all have "logs" to expunge. Circle below which ones may apply to you:

- Pride inhibits my ability to confess when I'm wrong.
- Insecurity creates false assumptions between me and others.
- Being a control freak makes it difficult to admit someone else has a better idea.
- Stubbornness invokes a strong-willed heart unwilling to relinquish power.
- Selfishness prevents me from seeing and caring for the needs of others.

There may be other logs seeking to build a cabin in our hearts. We all have them. Before we can remove them we must be willing to admit they exist. Spend some time in earnest reflection as you seek the Lord and ask His Spirit to reveal other areas you may not have recognized before. His Spirit can enable you to burn these logs before any more construction takes place in your heart.

5. Instead of pointing a finger at others, let's point others toward Christ. How does Jesus' example in John 8, of stooping and not slaying the sinner motivate you?

6. What will be required of your heart before you can confront someone's wrong? Why and whom do you feel justified to address and when does Scripture say this is permissible?

Bottom line, we should first look to examine ourselves in the light of Christ before seeking to perform surgery on someone else. Remember the warning from James 2:13, "*Judgment without mercy will be shown to anyone who has not been merciful.*" Unlike the Pharisees, we should point a finger at ourselves as we point to Christ to discard our trash. Then, we can accurately see our weaknesses for what they really are. This reality will keep us desperate for Christ. This recognition will also keep us contrite and repentant, not allowing ourselves to be elevated above anyone. And, when necessary, we will be equipped to handle cumbersome circumstances involving others with grace and humility.

Day 4: Free To Live

Confronting sin is obviously not the only time people feel judged. It could be experienced by an off-hand comment on a recent purchase or a questioning glance over someone's clothing or tattoos. Judgmental attitudes can arise when people disagree over areas of Christian freedom—another hot topic for today. I'm batting 1,000 aren't I? This is definitely an area where the see-saw can get completely off balance between legalism and grace, because everyone has an opinion about what is right for them, right?

Freedom in Christ is biblical, yet there are times we can abuse our Christian freedom for the sake of indulging our own fleshly desires. This can also precipitate pre-meditated grace. We deceive ourselves by claiming, "*Enjoy the moment, I'll just ask for forgiveness later.*" Or, because we fail to accurately understand biblical freedom we erroneously think, "*What's right for me is right for me, and I'll do it, enjoy it, read it, buy it, eat it, watch it, listen to it, wear it, drink it, etc., whenever and wherever I please, regardless.*" This selfishness neglects to put the needs of a weaker brother or sister in Christ first and ultimately fails to honor God.

Me-centered living also fails to embrace why we are free to live in Christ. We are free to live in Christ because of the gospel. Everything we do and every choice we make boils down to this central truth: the Gospel of Christ. There are lots of things we *can* do, but shouldn't. As Paul says, ***"Everything is permissible but not everything is beneficial. Everything is permissible but not everything is constructive"*** (1 Corinthians10:23). Our liberty is not a license for lawlessness or lack of love. We need to evaluate how much we are willing to experience *or* restrain from for the furtherance of the gospel. This is not about situational ethics either. Different situations may require a different response but undoubtedly there are uncompromising biblical truths that must always be upheld, no matter the circumstance.

Freedom is never free. We too easily forget how our freedom to live cost Jesus His life. The price He willingly paid should remind us of the true expense behind our choices. The blood of Jesus Christ paid for our spiritual freedom. Christ broke the chains of bondage and slavery to the Law, offering us the gift of grace and freedom from the penalty and power of sin. This truth is significant.

In both of these passages Paul is addressing Christian freedom, doing all to the glory of God with thanksgiving, acting in love and living by faith. Mutual acceptance of the weaker and stronger brothers without passing judgment or causing another to stumble is also addressed.

Remember, the Jews had strict laws governing their food choices (Leviticus 11; Deuteronomy 14) and Sabbath observance (Exodus 20:1-17). In 1 Corinthians, Paul declares no meat is unclean and is therefore permissible for consumption. However, a weaker brother may stumble when witnessing a stronger believer consume meat the weaker one has decided is unfit. Neither of them should look down on the other. In Romans Paul assures his audience not to question the history of meat when it is served by an unbeliever. But rather, partake with thankfulness to God, and whatever is done should be done in faith to His glory.

Day 4

> *Romans 14:7-8*
>
> *[7]For none of us lives to himself alone and none of us dies to himself alone. [8]If we live, we live to the Lord; and if we die, we die to the Lord. So, whether we live or die, we belong to the Lord.*

Romans 14:7-8 declares that in life or death we do not belong to ourselves; we belong to the Lord. This truth is fundamental in guiding choices within our Christian liberty. Instead of passing judgment on our brother's choices we are instructed to never put a stumbling block or hindrance in his way. It is wrong for anyone to put an obstacle in the way of a fellow brother. If we remember we ultimately live for God, and not ourselves, we will be enabled to act in love with regard to the weakness of a brother and not malign the Gospel.

1. 1 Corinthians 10:31 says, *"Whatever you do, do it all for the ______________ ______________________________ ."* How do we do this and what does this mean?

___

___

___

___

♡ *Heart Exam*

2. First-century issues with meat may not be relevant for us today, but there are plenty of things that do pertain to our culture and faith. Write down as many areas of Christian freedom as you can think of. Think broad and specific. (Some of these may even stem from deeply held convictions, traditions, or expectations we were raised with.)

___

___

___

Consider these possible scenarios:

- You are aware your Christian brothers struggle with being visually stimulated. Do you resist filtering your wardrobe for items that might reveal just too much skin, straps, lines or tightness?
- While having a dinner party you are aware a guest has just completed a 12-step recovery program for alcohol. Do you remove the wine that you are free to enjoy?
- An evening out with friends has you in line to buy movie tickets that might cross the line of what's acceptable to you. Do you openly discuss what R-rated movies (if any) are okay and what are not?
- Your friend just celebrated her 20th anniversary in the Bahamas. Are you excited for her or do you inwardly judge their spending and casually bring up your church's mission trip?
- You wouldn't dare let a drop of alcohol touch your tongue. But, when a seeking friend treats you to dinner she insists that you try her favorite alcoholic beverage. How do you respond?
- You are convinced Sunday is only for church. Your friend shares their family's recent hike in the mountains and their wonderful time with the Lord. Do you question her or share joy in their time of worship away from the church building?

3. Name an area or two that you know would be a stumbling block for a fellow brother or sister in Christ, but is not for you. How does your responsibility as a weaker or stronger brother, based on the preceding passages, influence your decision in helping protect them from falling?

4. Understanding what Christ did for you on the cross impacts your exercise of spiritual freedom. You don't want to abuse this freedom. From what you've learned in Romans and 1 Corinthians, how can your life reflect a biblical understanding of this delicate subject? Is your heart eager to please God or yourself? Are there any areas where you might be seeking to justify ungodly behavior?

To summarize Pope John Paul II, *"Freedom consists not in doing what we like, but in having the right to do what we ought."* [1] In his article *Let Freedom Ring* Rick Ezell says, *"Christian freedom is freedom from sin, not freedom to sin."* [2] God freed us from the penalty of sin, but it is our choice to live according to the principles of His Word.

In John 8:32, Jesus tells His disciples, *"Then you will know the truth and the truth will set you free."* Then, in John 8:36 tells us, *"If the Son sets you free, you will be free indeed."* Later John 14:6 says, *"I am the way, the truth and the life. No one comes to the Father except through me."* Ezell says later in his article, *"God's method for freedom is truth. When we believe the devil's lies and obey them, we experience bondage. God's purpose for us is freedom and God's method for freedom is truth. Freedom is life controlled by truth and motivated by love."* [3]

Freedom is the chance for us to become what God intends for His glory. While we operate under grace, our spiritual freedom is not a license to do whatever we want when we want. Spiritual freedom should bring us to a place of greater maturity because we recognize our responsibility as Christians.

Spiritual freedom should bring us to a place of greater maturity because we recognize our responsibility as Christians.

Consider these verses:

2 Corinthians 3:17 *"Now the Lord is the Spirit, and where the Spirit of the Lord is, there is freedom."*

---

1 *http://www.brainyquote.com/quotes/quotes/p/popejohnpa178860.html (accessed 2-28-13).*

2 *Let Freedom Ring by Rick Ezell. "The Lookout," Issue 27, July 4, 2010.*

3 *Ibid.*

Day 4

Galatians 5:1 *"It is for freedom that Christ has set us free; stand firm, then, and do not let yourselves be burdened again by a yoke of slavery."*

Galatians 5:13 *"Do not use your freedom to indulge the sinful nature; rather, serve one another in love."*

Sometimes my boys will ask, *"Why can't we do that? What's wrong with it?"* I turn the question around on them and say, *"What is right with it?" or "How is it good?"* Sometimes Christians tend to ask the same questions. We try to inwardly justify behavior we know is not right. It's like the teenagers who wonder how far they can sexually go and still be okay. This reveals a heart wanting to get away with something as long as it fits in the right box of "okay's." The problem is that once again we are faced with a Pharisaical choice. Do we partake in something based on a technicality of "rightness" or do we abstain, knowing it is unholy for what we claim to be as a Christ follower? Settling for degrees of wrongness seeks to justify ungodly behavior.

Our standard for righteousness and holy living must come from Truth, not our opinions. Right and holy living means that our thoughts, our attitudes, our actions and our words, should line up with the Word of God. *"God's instructions and boundaries aren't cruel barriers to keep me from freedom. They are protective restrictions meant to define where safe freedom can be found."* [4]

Next time we ask, "What is wrong with this?" We should instead ask ourselves these questions:

- † What is right with this?
- † Will this draw me closer to God?
- † Will this glorify Him?
- † Is this God's best for my life?
- † Am I trying to prove something by doing this?
- † Will this cause another brother or sister to stumble?
- † Is this a distraction from what God has called me to do?

Settling for degrees of wrongness seeks to justify ungodly behavior.

5. From what you have learned in today's lesson, what things may you need to reconsider about participating in or changing?

4 *"When My Wild Heart Pushes The Boundary," by Lysa Terkeurst January 28, 2013. https://mail.google.com/mail/u/0/#search/proverbs+encouragement/13c853d3eb6f76f1 (accessed 3-1-2013).*

Day 4

6. Share an area of Christian freedom you have experienced growth in. Meaning, maybe something you thought was wrong before, but in time God has matured you to a place of greater freedom. Or, something you have always done but not realized the potential stumbling block it may be to another.

7. How is the see-saw of legalism and grace becoming more balanced in your life?

Jesus was free from the legalistic measures the Pharisees imposed. Their religious bondage pigeonholed spiritual freedom for everyone. We've already learned the shackles they wore with the religious traditions of men and the numerous additions they made to the Law. Jesus came to free the nation of Israel from this captivity. The Pharisees failed to experience freedom in Christ because they neglected to embrace His teaching. We will, too, if we inaccurately presume to be above Christ's instructions. Instead of living by the letter of the Law, which brings death, let's live by the spirit of the law, which gives life (2 Corinthians 3:6). As Christians, we should truly celebrate our freedom in Christ. Remember though, our freedom is not free.

Day 5: Unity of Grace & Truth

For our final lesson this week, we'll dive below the surface of a widely misunderstood and often abused topic. Even though we have already brushed up on this, I'll attempt to paint a more compelling canvas of God's glorious favor. Grace. Our comprehension of this subject is reflected by how we live. Accurately living under God's grace will impact our relationship with God, others and ourselves. Living under an inaccurate understanding adversely affects these relationships as well.

Grace has been defined as God's riches at Christ's expense. The Greek definition comes from the transliterated word *charis*, unmerited favor, or an undeserved gift. [1] Grace is not something we achieve, but rather a gift we receive. Christ broke cultural barriers to extend grace to others. This is seen by how He loved, healed, forgave sin and ultimately died on the cross. His example and ability to offer such charity bugged the anti-grace Pharisees. They neglected to accept Jesus' grace.

Grace is not something we achieve, but rather a gift we receive.

Consider these verses:

Galatians 2:21 *"I do not set aside the grace of God, for if righteousness could be obtained through the law, Christ died for nothing."*

Ephesians 2:8-9 *"For it is by grace you have been saved, through faith-and this not from yourselves, it is the gift of God-not by works, so that no one can boast."*

2 Timothy 1:8b-10 *"God, who has saved us and called us to a holy life-not because of anything we have done but because of his own purpose and grace. This grace was given us in Christ Jesus before the beginning of time, but it has now been revealed through the appearing of our Savior, Christ Jesus, who has destroyed death and has brought life and immortality to light through the gospel."*

Accurately comprehending grace embraces the truth that we don't earn our salvation and we are not repaying God by good works. Faulty belief will strive to perform in order to gain God's approval through human effort. What should be a response of gratitude is replaced with obligation. This can easily occur in our "you get what you pay for" society. Nothing is free—except for maybe getting sick. Grace is no longer grace if we're working for something that is already free.

Grace is no longer grace if we're working for something that is a gift.

Failure to understand grace also impacts our relationship with others. When we live biblically under His grace, we are more apt to extend this grace to others. When we live in a state of grace, it allows us to forgive more easily because we know that others need to experience what we have received. We also won't expect of others what we don't expect of ourselves. Grace enables us to release the grip of confinement and relinquish our tendency to control situations.

---

1 *http://www.blueletterbible.org/lang/lexicon/lexicon.cfm?Strongs=G5485&t=NASB (accessed 3-4-2013).*

Walking in Christ's grace-filled grasp enables us to embrace each day with confidence. While we know mistakes are inevitable, our assurance of His grace covers us. This allows us to live unhindered, without wondering when the guillotine will be released. This certainty compels us to also live rightly without scorning His grace or abusing our freedom. As Paul says in Romans 6:1, *"Shall we go on sinning so that grace may increase? By no means! We died to sin; how can we live in it any longer?"*

1. What other ways would you say living under God's grace positively or negatively impacts your relationship with God, yourself and others?

Don't misunderstand, a person can accept the blood of Christ as payment for their sin and be born again. And, the fruit of their life can even look beautiful, but beneath the surface the seed of legalism tries to take root. Maybe when others taste this fruit they experience judgment, harshness and self-exaltation. I lived like this for a time. As I mentioned last week, the enemy is crafty in his attempt to help us assume we can somehow partner with God in the business of our salvation by grace.

> I knew I was a sinner in need of Christ. I eagerly ran to Him and embraced His love and forgiveness. But for years I did not grasp the concept of grace. I tried so hard to do the "right things" and live the "right way," often based on others' expectations of me. They weren't necessarily wrong, but I somehow mistakenly thought that I had to keep my end of the bargain in order to remain acceptable in the eyes of God. I began to take false pride in my righteous life and looked at others like they were the ones who simply "didn't get it." How ironic that I was the one who actually "didn't get it."
>
> While I was in college I took the Bible class Romans. This was a spiritual journey I would never forget. It wasn't long before my professor hammered the class on grace, grace and more grace. What I learned through this nine-month pilgrimage revolutionized my relationship with God because I began to accept my salvation by faith and truly live under His grace, which not only impacted my relationship with the Lord, but also profoundly corrected the lens I viewed others through.

Day 5

Take a moment to review your response from Day 1 (page 60) to the same see-saw below and see how God has been working in your heart. Hopefully you have been able to work through some of your weaknesses related to legalism and grace, and you are experiencing a more biblical approach in your relationship with God and others. Mark below where you presently sit on the see-saw.

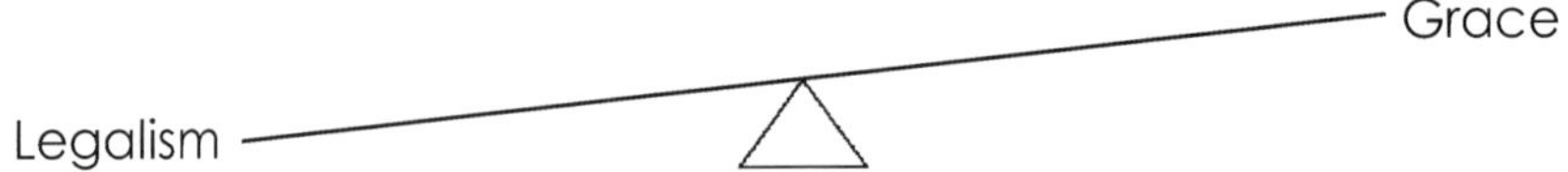

Biblical balance is necessary and growth takes time. This is not a quick fix, but a call to evaluate our present reality and make necessary changes that will strengthen our faith and daily commitment to Christ.

2. Based on what you have learned this week, what has helped you to grow in this area? What has impacted you the most from the lessons this week?

Read John 1:14-17

This passage is not suggesting that the Law was bad and Jesus is good. Both play a significant role in the history of salvation. The Law graciously revealed the righteous requirements for the nation of Israel. Jesus' entrance marked the final revelation of God's complete redemptive work of grace and truth.[2] Jesus is the complete embodiment of grace and truth.

This grace and truth was rejected by the Pharisees. Walking according to God's grace and truth can be tricky. Sometimes it may be easier to walk in truth and not grace. Remember, the Pharisees had the truth and knowledge of the Scriptures, yet failed to embrace grace. This adversely impacted their relationship with God and others.

As we've studied this week, the flip side of this could be walking in grace to the extent that truth is abandoned. These two theological aspects are not mutually exclusive. We cannot readily experience or accurately embrace one without the other. To do so would catapult us off the see-saw. We need God's truth and His grace to be spiritually balanced. To keep the see-saw level, legalism and strict adherence or judgment of others must return to truth. Grace must reject the "prove-self" life and accept redemption with a blank resumé.

2 *ESV Study Bible, Crossway Bibles 2008, p. 2020.*

Colossians 1:5-6 states, *"The faith and love that spring from the hope that is stored up for you in heaven and that you have already heard about in the word of truth, the gospel that has come to you. All over the world this gospel is bearing fruit and growing, just as it has been doing among you since the day you heard it and understood God's grace in all its truth."*

The word of truth claimed in Colossians is the Gospel of Christ: His death, burial and resurrection. Because we carry the death of Christ in us, being touched by grace is not easily forgotten. According to this passage, understanding God's grace in all its truth will result in fruitful multiplication of the gospel message. The opposite is also true: the gospel is hindered when we don't accurately comprehend—hopefully, we are beginning to understand the implications of accurately living in grace and truth.

3. How does this impact your relationship with others and with God?

Legalism twists truth and abuses grace. Freedom embraces truth and expresses grace. Grace knows truth and truth lives in love. When the enemy tempts us to sway to one side or the other we need to remember the importance of maintaining our position in Christ and the unity of God's grace and truth. May we strive to live balanced on the often imbalanced see-saw.

Oh Lord, this week has been heavy. I recognize areas in my heart I desperately need You to heal. I feel imbalanced with the grace I extend to others and sometimes struggle with exercising my Christian "rights," yet fail to consider my fellow sister or brother in Christ. Please help me be more aware of others' needs before my own and to be mindful of my motives. I want to reflect the Gospel through my life. Thank You for enabling me as I yield in these areas.

In Your Mighty Name,
Amen.

VIEWER GUIDE

WEEK THREE

Titus 2:11-14; Romans 6:15-18; 1 Corinthians 10:23 -11:1; Romans 14:1-23; 1 Corinthians 8:7-13; Galatians 5:13; Exodus 21:2-6

Four ways we can become judgmental:

1. Looking at everyone else and ________________ our life to theirs.
2. Base our expectations on how we think others should be __________ .
3. Impose our ______ - ________ ____________ onto others.
4. We don't know the shoes others walk in so we make faulty _____________________ .

Legalism is _______________ - ____________ It seeks to ____________ man-made rules and earn the favor of God or others while appearing to be extra-spiritual.

__________________ to God's Word is not legalism. (Titus 2:11-14; Philippians 3:7; Ephesians 5:33; 6:4; 2 Corinthians 5:17; Romans 6:2; 12:2; Mark 8:34-35; Deuteronomy 6:6-9; 1 Corinthians 6:18-20)

As Christians we are free to live — not how we want or how we like — but rather, we are free to live ________________________ .

A Slave *(doulos)* is "one who __________ _______________ _____ to another's will – those whose service is used by Christ in extending and advancing His cause among men." [1]

We are free . . . yet, we are ___________ .

We have a _____________________ to our fellow brother's/sister's; to serve them in love.

We would be wise to model the example of Paul concerning our Christian freedoms:

1. Do what leads to peace and mutual edification — by accepting those who are _____________ without passing judgment.
2. Do everything to the ________ of God — by responding with thankfulness and in faith by what we do.
3. Seek the good of others instead of our own good — by putting others interests ________ , not ours.
4. Act in ________ by not putting a stumbling block in their way — and by removing what may hinder them.

WHY? So they may be ________ **.** (1 Corinthians 9:19; 10:33; 11:1; Philippians 2:7).
For the furtherance of the ____________ **!**

Exodus 21:2-6 [2]

Let's remove the logs from our eyes, and instead, focus on the Master who has ____________ ______ _____ .

WEEK FOUR

"U" Comes Before "I"

Day 1

Exalt Who?

Day 2

The Insecurity of Pride Cheats

Day 3

The Great Teacher

Day 4

Blinded & Questioning

Day 5

Just Like Jesus

WEEK FOUR—"U" COMES BEFORE "I"

Day 1: Exalt Who?

Since the beginning of time, pride found itself in the hearts of men, beginning with Adam and Eve. They circumvented God's authority and made a choice based on their own desires and greeds. They appointed themselves above God by thinking their ways were higher than His and that their enlightenment exceeded God's best for them. Painful consequences followed their prideful fall.

We'll embark on a spiritual journey this week as we investigate pride and humility. Our exploration will take us into the crevices of our hearts needing repair and to the rough edges that need smoothed. Recognizing the pitfalls of pride will enable us to better exemplify a life of humility, where, as the word "humility" reveals, "U" comes before "I." This kind of life embraces internal purity over external piety. Once again, we'll learn valuable insight from Jesus and His dealings with the Pharisees. They unashamedly exuded what Christ unwaveringly criticized.

None of us are exempt from the poison of pride. Depending on the situation this toxin may present itself in unlikely ways. This infection contaminates and decays our hearts while it seeks to elevate self and exalt personal ego. Interestingly, right smack in the middle of P-R-I-D-E is "I." "I" is the main ingredient of this deadly venom.

When we are full of ourselves we swallow the sickness that wages war within us and we experience the results of living a prideful life. A person full of self is empty spiritually because Christlikeness cannot develop in an environment of personal glorification. The root of pride is self. Pride is an undue sense of one's own superiority. This is different from possessing a proper sense of personal dignity and worth. I am talking about elevating ourselves above others, showing contempt towards them, having a superior view of ourselves, or the tendency to look out for our own interests instead of those of others.

Pride manifests itself in various ways: selfishness, insecurity, self-reliance, conceit, stubbornness, self-righteousness, vanity, arrogance, being easily threatened, experiencing shallow relationships and self-preservation, etc.

Pride resists submission to any governing authority because pride encourages people to be their own boss. Ultimately, a person cannot sincerely surrender to Christ without submitting to His authority. But, let's say we have placed ourselves under Christ's Lordship and accepted Him as Savior. The fatality of pride can still creep into our hearts, virtually hindering every aspect of our lives. Pride's illusive power and temptation to exalt self will strangle us spiritually if we don't intentionally release its grip by subduing our flesh.

Day 1

♡ ***Heart Exam***

1. No one is exempt from the temptation to be full of themselves. How does pride manifest itself in your life? What results are currently evident in your life?

2. Maybe you are in the midst of battling spiritual emptiness. Have you considered that you might be full of the wrong things? Reflect and share what the Lord is teaching you through this time.

In addition, elevating ourselves decreases our exaltation of Christ. Promoting self diminishes our Savior. We cannot bully God for His throne, *but* we can bow. In contrast, when Christ remains the center of our lives, we experience the fruit of a life repelled by the grasp of pride. And, when we are full of Him, we become emptier of self. As G.K. Chesterton says, "*How much larger would your life be if yourself could become smaller in it?*" [1]

James 4:6 tells us, ***"But he gives us more grace. That is why Scripture says: 'God opposes the proud but gives grace to the humble.' "*** The word for oppose (*antitassomai*) means to do battle against or resist. [2] God battles against and resists the proud but delivers grace to the humble because a humble person is not consumed with "self" interest. Privilege, entitlement and arrogance are the very antitheses of a life in Christ. Grace—an undeserved gift—can hardly be received when pride encompasses a heart.

The parable we'll look at today is one of my favorites. It seems ridiculous that someone would actually do such a thing. But, the reality is that Jesus uses this teaching to show this is exactly how the Pharisees lived and behaved towards others. Even though time and circumstances may be different, we have the propensity to react the same way today.

1 Orthodoxy, G.K. Chesterton. Waterbrook Press, Colorado Springs, CO. © 1994, 2001. p. 20.

2 http://classic.studylight.org/isb/view.cgi?number=498 (accessed 3-5-13).

Day 1

Read Luke 18:9-14

3. What does the Pharisee's prayer reveal about the condition of his heart? If he did so many right things, what was wrong?

4. According to verse 13, the tax collector had a posture and position of humility. What does Ezra 9:6 reveal about the condition of the heart when one is unable to lift up their face before God?

> *Ezra 9:6*
>
> *[6]and prayed: O my God, I am too ashamed and disgraced to lift up my face to you, my God, because our sins are higher than our heads and our guilt has reached to the heavens.*

5. What does the tax collector's prayer reveal about the state of his heart?

Verse 14 says, *"I tell you that this man [tax collector], rather than the other [Pharisee],* went home justified before God. Then Christ says, *"Everyone who exalts himself will be humbled, and he who humbles himself will be exalted."*

This is a great paradox: the exalted will be humbled and the humbled will be exalted. The Pharisee measured his value according to what he did and didn't do and who he wasn't like. His arrogance compelled him to eagerly boast of his achievements *and* he felt justified placing himself above this sinner.

6. Share a time when you have done something similar to this Pharisee. Or simply put, how have you completed this sentence: *"At least I'm not as bad as* ______________________." Maybe you weren't praying in church, but what thoughts have sprouted in your heart when you've been tempted to pride yourself compared to another sinner?

Day 1

7. Why is comparing our sins to others' sins or comparing our goodness to their goodness wrong?

Jesus uses great irony in this parable. Both men were sinners, but only one willingly acknowledged it. The Pharisees knew the tax collectors in the first century were dishonest thieves. More than likely this man pilfered others' pockets with exorbitant taxes and perhaps added a little cushion to his own wallet. He seeks God's mercy and recognizes his unworthiness. The Pharisee, obviously blind to his own deceit, has the audacity to brag about his 'number one' and appears to feel pretty good about it too. Here's a greater irony: the one lacking mercy—who sought justification—went home unjustified. And, the penitent one seeking mercy went home justified.

Proverbs 8:13

[13]To fear the LORD is to hate evil; I hate pride and arrogance, evil behavior and perverse speech.

> *Biblical scholar Adam Clarke says the following about the Pharisee: "He was abased, because he vainly trusted that he was righteous, and depended on what he had been enabled to do, and looked not for a change of heart, nor for reconciliation to God. It is a strange perversion of the human mind, to attempt to make God our debtor by the very blessings which his mere mercy has conferred upon us!"* [3]

"For whoever exalts himself will be humbled, and whoever humbles himself will be exalted" (Matthew 23:12). Proverbs 8:13 reminds us that God hates pride and arrogance. Maybe today we've been able to loosen the choke-hold of pride in our hearts. Perhaps we have gained greater clarity to its various manifestations in our lives. It's also possible that we recognize we've been exalting the wrong person. Is it now conceivable that it is time for us to humbly repent and cry out to God for mercy?

Lord Jesus, I praise You for Your Word that teaches me the importance of humility and warns me of the pitfalls of pride. I ask for Your Spirit to reveal to me the places in my heart that may be fostering a prideful response or reaction, self-exaltation or justification. Empty me of myself Lord, so that I can be filled with the power of Your presence and be untangled from the damaging knots of pride. I ask this in faith, Lord, desiring the blessings of Your grace and hungering for Your will above my own.

In Jesus' precious name I pray,
Amen.

3 *The Adam Clarke Commentary http://classic.studylight.org/com/acc/view.cgi?book=lu&chapter=018 (accessed 3-6-13).*

Day 2: The Insecurity of Pride Cheats

One of the symptoms of pride mentioned in Day 1 is insecurity. At first glance one may wonder how these two could even relate. Because I believe I am not the only woman who has ever had an issue with this, I would like to spend a portion of today showing the negative progression of how pride and insecurity cheat us.

The root to pride is self. If our self is not established in the value and worth of Christ, then our security is threatened. Prideful people are often insecure because pride causes confusion with our personal value and where we derive our worth. If our personal value can be made just a little bit higher in relation to others then we are obviously better than they are, so we think.

As we've learned, the Pharisees often proved their security and worth by measuring up to the Law. They were pretentious in their positions, performance and pedigree. If our worth and value are attached to our achievements our teeth will sink deeper into the fruit of deception, just like Eve in the Garden. Pride will no longer be like an unwanted stray cat, but rather a permanent pestilence.

Until we live in the truth that our value comes from Christ, we hurt the relationships we have with others because we always have to prove ourselves. Secretly, we may want others to look bad or not really succeed. Our insecurities also create exclusive versus inclusive friendships. And, a desire to appear elite over common, puffs up our expectations of others. This insecurity also engages the jealousy throttle into over-drive.

> When we were newlyweds our in-laws visited our little apartment. I took great pride in this special place, a little too much in fact. Everything was tidy and clean and all baking was done beforehand. We were ready for the white glove test. After dinner my sister-n-law and I washed dishes. She noticed that our stainless steel pans had accumulated some residue. She asked if I had an SOS pad, to which I said no. She insisted they would remove the nasty build-up, but I declared the pans were just fine. *Who needs SOS pads? Soap and water are all I need. I'll just scrub harder. Who is she to question how I wash dishes when she can't even keep her house clean? That would be like going to a dentist who has jungle rot in his teeth!*
>
> The next day she bought some SOS pads, brought them back to our apartment and proceeded to excitedly demonstrate, with the prior evening dishes, how easily they take off the scum. *Lovely.* Can you see my eyeballs rolling? In my arrogance, I was less than thrilled with another woman instructing me on how to properly clean my dishes. This little episode infuriated me because I thought she now had the upper hand, so to speak. I wanted to be better than she and my posture of perfection began to crumble. How could I admit someone else had a great idea or that I was wrong? My heart was clearly not in the right place. My haughtiness hindered our relationship. Eventually, I had to humble myself and finally admit I wasn't "all that." (I have since wised up. I'll have you know I cannot live without SOS pads!)

Day 2

A prideful and insecure person works with a negative and comparing mindset. With this mindset, one cannot think they are a winner, unless someone else is a loser. I win, you lose; you lose, I win. Their value is increased by winning or by others losing. A prideful person would rather see someone fail than succeed. For someone to succeed at something they haven't, means they're no good, or so they believe. Others' lack of success increases their self-worth. This faulty negative and comparing mindset assures them they are better than others.

This may sound a little "junior high-ish," but I assure you, adult women are guilty and victims of this as well. Even if we don't consider ourselves to be competitive, we can have secret agendas in our minds and hearts. The temptation is common and can be far reaching into all hearts. Pride can sneak its way into our lives in seemingly innocent and sly ways. Galatians 5:26 exhorts, ***"Let us not become conceited, provoking and envying each other."***

Circle below which examples resonate with you:

- Parenting becomes a competition: *Johnny is still not sleeping through the night and he's four months old. Or, He's still not potty trained. Or, I'm so glad my kids are not like theirs. I would never let my kids do that . . . watch that . . . eat that . . . wear that . . . say that!*
- Being better at something than someone else fuels the fire of pride. Why don't we just walk around with our resumés taped to our foreheads so everyone knows how great we've become? Promotions and status make us feel important.
- Friendships are destroyed because personal insecurities can cause envy or judgment on another. *I would look that good too if I could afford the spa membership and personal trainer. She always thinks she has the answer for everything! I sure wish I could have an ounce of her talent.*

♡ Heart Exam

We all have various issues of pride and insecurity needing to be dealt with in our hearts. After reflecting on today's lesson, pray about those weak places where you need His aid.

1. From what you've learned so far today, what impacts you the most about pride and insecurity?

2. How does the source of your derived self-worth affect your relationships with others? Based on your answer, try to identify whether you possess inclusive or exclusive friendships.

3. A negative mindset can be connected to raging insecurities. How does your jealousy throttle get engaged? Of whom are you jealous and to whom are you tempted to compare yourself?

A heart filled with arrogance is easily irritated by anything it cannot control or dominate. My friend Sherrie reminded me how we like to categorize people in an effort to minimize them. *They are weak, strong, introverted, busy, lazy, talented, challenged, flaky, committed, sweet, sour, shallow, insecure*... and the list goes on. When we label people like this it is often a ploy to heighten ourselves in order to steamroll another. This way, we don't have to deal with our own weaknesses.

> God taught this lesson to me one summer morning while leading a ladies' study at the local city park. There was a woman who, in my judgmental and prideful opinion, was high-maintenance and shallow. Her external appearance was so put together, while I was lucky to just get a shower in the rush of the morning. In my mind, and unknown to others, I hastily labeled her this way and doubted her spiritual depth.
>
> But through the course of the summer God helped me see a deeper side of this woman as she slowly opened her heart. She loved God and was hungry for more of Him. She needed to be discipled, loved and befriended by godly women. Honestly, who cares that she looked nicer than I did for a Bible study in the park. The truth is, I failed to manage my time at home and appeared thrown together as I was. I was also partially jealous she had more fashionable clothing than I did, which revealed discontent in my heart. But I was quick to assume that if she had the time to look nice on the outside then she must not be as spiritually groomed on the inside. The Lord gave me quite a spiritual spanking for being so rash in labeling her unfairly.

In the case of the SOS pads, I was threatened by my sister-in-law. My personal value was challenged when I wouldn't accept a better idea from someone else. My sense of worth and why I am valuable was not backed up with the truth of God's love for me. I forgot that I have no need to ever justify myself. Although I claim to worship God, in this example I worshiped myself. All who worship themselves do not have a clear comprehension of who they really are in Christ. By doing so, they bulldoze God to the side while trying to walk on stilts above everyone else.

Read Luke 20:45-47 (Notice the six things Jesus states the teachers of the Law like to do.)

Day 2

Read Matthew 23:5-7 (Notice the additional four things Jesus mentions here.)

4. What do these items reveal about the Pharisees?

____

____

____

> *Matthew 23:5-7*
>
> *[5]Everything they do is done for men to see: They make their phylacteries wide and the tassels on their garments long; [6]they love the place of honor at banquets and the most important seats in the synagogues; [7]they love to be greeted in the marketplaces and to have men call them 'Rabbi.'*

Jesus warns against their lives of show. Their deeds were done for men to see. Can you imagine the parade, pomp and circumstance? They cherished wearing special garments that set them apart. They sought honor instead of humility. They took advantage of the needy. They desired positions of importance. Their prayers were for people and not for God. And they loved to hear others call out their title. Whether they were dressing, sitting, walking, eating, worshiping or celebrating, they solicited special treatment and visibility. They cheated themselves by living such a counterfeit life. Their foundation for security in Christ eroded because their lives were built around performance.

5. What the Pharisees loved, Jesus loathed. Is it any wonder Jesus declares in Luke 20:47, *"Such men will be ______________________________."* Let those words sink in for a minute.

Now let's consider what Jesus might say to us in the 21st century. There could be similar accolades we eagerly desire. After all, a performing heart is ready for the show. This heart of arrogance welcomes applause, appearance, achievement and exaltation.

6. Based on the present condition of your heart, what would Jesus say to you? *Beware of (your name) she likes ______________________________. Such ladies will be punished most severely.* This is an example of how pride cheats us.

Let's consider other ways pride can cheat us. Beth Moore says this about pride: **My name is Pride. I am a Cheater.** [1] Circle those that resonate with you. Beth says this about pride:

- I cheat you of your God-given destiny because you demand your own way.
- I cheat you of contentment because you "deserve better" than this.
- I cheat you of knowledge because you already "know it all."
- I cheat you of healing because you are too full of "Me" to forgive.
- I cheat you of holiness because you refuse to admit when you are wrong.
- I cheat you of vision because you would rather look in the mirror than out the window.

---

1 *Praying God's Word – Breaking Free from Spiritual Strongholds, Beth Moore. Broadman & Holman Publishers, © 2009. p. 38-40.*

Day 2

- I cheat you of genuine friendship because nobody is ever going to know the real you.
- I cheat you of love because REAL romance demands a sacrifice.
- I cheat you of greatness in Heaven because you refuse to wash somebody else's feet here on earth.
- I cheat you of God's glory because I've convinced you that you better seek your own glory.
- I am pride and I am a cheater. You like me because you think I am always looking out for you but that is so untrue. I am looking to make a fool out of you.
- God has so much for you, but as long as you stick with me (pride), you'll never know.

While reading this list maybe the Lord revealed other areas of pride in your life. It's important to recognize seeds of arrogance and how they might be nurtured in your heart. If left unchecked, the seed will sprout weeds and inhibit your spiritual growth.

7. Share your thoughts below and any new weak places the Lord brought to mind.

Read Luke 14:7-14

8. This passage is similar to what we've looked at today, but I want to key in on one specific outcome. What does verse 9 reveal as the result of the man looking for honor in this parable?

As Luke 14 teaches, seeking honor invites humiliation. It's time for our pride to be penetrated and replaced with humility of heart. Today's been heavy. Spend some extra time reflecting and praying over those private and painful places the Lord wants to purge from within you. In closing, hide in your heart 1 Peter 5:5b-6. *"All of you, clothe yourselves with humility toward one another, because, 'God opposes the proud but gives grace to the humble.' Humble yourselves, therefore, under God's mighty hand, that he may lift you up in due time."*

Day: 3 The Great Teacher

I was outside preparing to vacuum the inside of our van when my son approached and asked if I would try out his new "sweet" shoes, aka, Heelys. In my *humility*, I told him, *"Give me those goofy shoes with wheels and I'll show you how it's done, son."* As I tied the laces while humming "Footloose," I recalled my roller-skating glory days to my nine-year-old. I told him how I won the limbo championship, danced the hokey-pokey, and how I used to roller-skate backwards to "Old Time Rock-n-Roll."

I stood up with these "shoes" and quickly realized they were *nothing* like roller-skates. *Do I swallow my humble pie now or after I crash?* Let's just say, Heelys are not made for people in my age group—or coordination level. The manufacturers should put a disclaimer or caution tape around these death traps. Immediately Proverbs 16:18 echoed in my mind, *"Pride goes before destruction, a haughty spirit before a fall."* (You can stop laughing now.)

In our prior two lessons I emphasized how pride affects our relationship with God and others. This lesson will highlight the impact humility brings to our lives. Like pride, humility plays a significant role in our interaction with God and with others.

The word humble (*tapeinos*) is an adjective meaning to make low; to bow.[1] The humble person is not concerned with elevating himself. They are not self-centered or concerned about their status. C.S. Lewis says, *"Humility is not thinking less of yourself, but thinking of yourself, less."*[2] In truth, humility is the ongoing recognition of our position in relation to God *and* how we position ourselves in relation to others.

On Day 1 we looked at James 4:6, *"But he gives us more grace. That is why Scripture says: 'God opposes the proud but gives grace to the humble.' "* We questioned how grace can be received when our hearts are full of pride. Well, it can't. Several years ago I was on a personal journey to discover why humility is essential in my relationship with God. He had much to reveal to my sometimes stubborn and puffed up heart.

♡ ***Heart Exam***

1. Why is humility a necessary on-going component in our journey with God?

During an intense time of studying this passage in James He whispered, *"When you are truly humble, Hester, you will recognize My place of authority in your life . . . this is when you are TEACHABLE."* This insight unlocked many areas of frustration in my life at that point. Too often, I had plowed ahead of God or tried to convince Him of my plans or failed to receive instruction or correction

1 *http://www.blueletterbible.org/lang/lexicon/lexicon.cfm?Strongs=G5011&t=KJV (accessed 3-12-13).*
2 *http://www.brainyquote.com/quotes/authors/c/c_s_lewis.html (accessed 3-12-13).*

from another and then found myself irritated when things didn't turn out how I thought they should. When I am humble, I am teachable. I tuck this truism deep within my core.

God went on to show me the characteristics of a teachable heart. Teachable hearts are attentive to the Lord. They are eager to follow His lead and obey His instructions. They are willing to receive and respond to His rebuke, discipline *and* correction from others. We hinder this teach-ability when we lack true humility.

2. What other characteristics of a teachable heart can you think of?

Negative results occur when we nurse a prideful heart. A heart full of pride is not teachable. Arrogance stands in the way of obedience to the Lord. Pride prohibits us from receiving and responding to His correction. This also inhibits our ability to confess when we are wrong or admit we have a need. A life vying for self is me-centered and leaves God out of the equation. Like a raging fire, pride devours; like a hydrant, humility extinguishes its consuming flames.

Read John 9:13-34 (More to come on this passage in tomorrow's lesson.)

3. Based on this passage, the Pharisees were not very teachable. Verse 34 reveals that they ultimately threw the man out. Now notice, in this discourse, who is asking all the questions? What is it about this man's answers the Pharisees do not like?

4. Why were the Pharisees unwilling to be taught or lectured by this man? What was their problem?

Day 3

5. Remember, the Pharisees were experts in the Law. What did their expertise fail to consider?

The Pharisees normally sneered at Jesus' teaching because it targeted weak places in their souls. They were often wrong and unwilling to admit this. They did not like being the poster child for how "not" to live. Now, they are faced with a healed blind man, and their response is no different. Their haughtiness hid any attempt of humility.

When we fail to live humble lives, we unavoidably shut God out by not being teachable disciples. This truly is an oxymoron because a disciple is a doing learner; one who puts into practice what he knows to be true and have learned. When we are not teachable we lose the opportunity to learn from God, grow in Him and to be transformed into His likeness.

An unknown author says, "*Jesus was a walking scalpel, set upon the earth with love and deft wisdom to prune away the hate and the pride and the poison out of your human heart and mine; if we will let Him.*"

In response to yesterday's list, "My Name is Pride. I am a Cheater," by Beth Moore, the Lord prompted me to develop a similar list regarding humility: **"My Name Is Humility. I Am A Teacher."** Circle those that resonate with you:

- I teach you how to celebrate over others' accomplishments because you acknowledge you are not in competition with them and you can admit they are deserving of such honor.
- I teach you how to serve others and put them before yourself because you understand you are not created to serve yourself or have a life of entitlement because of Christ's example.
- I teach you to apologize when you are wrong and ask for forgiveness because you are willing to admit your mistakes and you understand the importance of making amends and maintaining unity.
- I teach you not to judge others because you know you have your own issues of sin and therefore, are no better than anyone.
- I teach you your weaknesses because it helps you recognize your need for Jesus.
- I teach you about righteousness because you hunger for God and His word.
- I teach you to respect authority because you are surrendered to the Lordship of Christ.
- I teach you to recognize your sin because you need to be reminded that you cannot save yourself.
- I teach you where your true value comes from because you can confess there's no need to compare or be jealous of others because your worth is established in Christ.

Day 3

- I teach you about love because it is the greatest attribute for you to possess.
- My name is Humility and I am a Teacher. You love me because I keep your relationship with God healthy. You want me around because I manage to suppress your ego enough for you to bow at the feet of Christ.
- God has amazing things in store for you. As long as you stick with me, Humility, you will always grow.

When we are humble, then we are teachable.

6. Friends, when we are humble, we are teachable. Spend some time reflecting how humility gives you a teachable heart and allows God to show you Himself and His ways. Pray and meditate on the truths you have gleaned today. Share how else humility teaches you.

Isaiah 66:2b, "*This is the one I esteem: he who is humble and contrite in spirit, and trembles at my word.*" Being exalted in God's kingdom will result from being humble. Matthew 23:12 also teaches, ***"For whoever exalts himself will be humbled, and whoever humbles himself will be exalted."*** Or, in other words, *"Whoever exalts himself will be lowered."* May we never shun the great teacher, humility.

Day 4: Blinded & Questioning

It is vital to understand how humility is a key component when we choose to accept Christ and follow Him. Pride often keeps people from surrendering to Christ. They are unwilling to kneel before a new governing authority and admit they actually need God. They would rather live independently of God.

Humility allows us to accept God's position by submitting to His Lordship. Humility opens our eyes to our weaknesses and unworthiness which allows us to see our desperate need for Jesus. Humility also enables us to recognize our sin for what it is, in light of Who God is. Nancy Leigh DeMoss says, *"When we gaze upon the brilliance of God's untarnished holiness, we become acutely aware of the hideousness of our sin and the smallness of our greatness."* [1] This realization should bear the fruit of repentance in our lives.

When humility is decreased, so is our spiritual vision. When we are spiritually blinded, questioning God's authority will increase. The Pharisees were notorious for calling the authority of Jesus into question (Mark 8:11; 11:28; Luke 20:2; Matthew 16:1; 21; 23; John 2:18). Somehow, if they could discredit this Nazarene, then their image would not be tarnished. Nor would they have to abide by this so-called rabbi's teaching, or respect His authority. Jesus was radical. He wasn't one of them. He failed to offer the applause they admired. He called out their false teaching multiple times. Following Christ's leadership was the Pharisees' most unlikely ambition. Ultimately, they plotted how they could kill Him.

Today we will continue to examine the startling effects of neglecting to exercise humility in our lives. We will follow-up with the passage in John 9 again in order to drive home a deeper point regarding spiritual blindness.

Notice the order:

V. 15 – The Pharisees ask about the blind man's healing. The blind man answered.

V. 16 – The Pharisees discredit Jesus.

V. 17 – The Pharisees ask the blind man his opinion of Jesus. The blind man answered, "He must be a prophet."

V. 18 – The Jewish leaders still refuse to believe the man was born blind. The Pharisees call in the man's parents to verify.

V. 20 – The parents verify his blindness from birth, but don't proclaim Christ as Messiah. They tell the leaders to question their son about the matter.

V. 24 – The Pharisees discredit Jesus, again.

V. 26 – The Pharisees ask the blind man again about his healing.

---

1 *Lies Women Believe and the Truth That Sets Them Free, Moody Publishers, 2001. p. 100*

V. 27 – The blind man is frustrated at the Pharisees' lack of understanding. He's already told them the truth. He doesn't repeat the story. He asks if the Pharisees want to become Jesus' disciples.

V. 28 – The Pharisees curse the blind man and discredit Jesus again.

V. 30 – The blind man sees through the Pharisees' blindness. The blind man acknowledges Jesus must be from God.

V. 34 – The Pharisees discredit the blind man and excommunicate him from the synagogue.

1. If you look closely you will notice that the Pharisees tried to discredit the blind man multiple times in this chain of events. What does this reveal about the stubborn pride in the Pharisees' hearts?

2. The Pharisees were faced with truth yet they undermined the truth repeatedly. What would accepting the truth have meant for their lives?

Verse 27 reveals an irritated once-blind man. The Pharisees start in with the same litany of questions this man already answered. Perhaps their intent is to confuse him and rebut such favor towards this man named Jesus. This reminds me of my boys who ask me a question, but because they don't like my answer they ask again in hopes of getting a different answer. To which I sometimes feel like saying, *"C'mon, you heard me the first time. Were ya' listening?"*

> *"The man born blind knows his interrogators have no thought of becoming Jesus' disciples, but his ironical question is used by the Evangelist as a means of introducing again the subject of true discipleship."* [2]

The Pharisees respond by affirming that Moses was their leader—No one doubted God spoke to Moses because they knew Old Testament Scriptures. Their claim as Moses' disciples made sense because they were. They failed to accept Jesus Christ as the complete revelation of God, in addition to the Law being delivered through Moses. The Pharisees knew the Messiah was coming, but they resisted embracing that Christ was He. Jesus did not fit into their pint-size box of what the King of Kings should be like.

The once-blind man speaks again and begins to emphatically state truths about God. He states the obvious, or what should appear plain to those present. This doesn't go over so well with the trained professionals. They start to feel the heat of losing this argument. These leaders reject this man's claims and furthermore discredit him.

---

2 *The Gospel of John, F.F. Bruce. William B. Eerdmans Publishing Company, 1983. p. 217.*

Day 4

Read John 9:35-41

Heart Exam

3. This section is the response of Christ to John 9:13-34, where Jesus teaches a greater truth regarding blindness. How else was the man born blind healed?

4. Jesus indicts the Pharisees in verses 39-41. According to Jesus' pronouncement in these verses, what is the end result of not only their spiritual blindness but of anyone rejecting Christ?

5. How has your spiritual vision been impaired and how have your eyes been opened?

6. Healed vision shares boldly. The man born blind courageously spoke of his changed life both physically and spiritually. How eager are you to share your story? Why or why not?

Matthew 15:14

14 Leave them; they are blind guides. If a blind man leads a blind man, both will fall into a pit.

Day 4

7. What were the consequences the man born blind faced for boldly speaking? (It was the same fear his parents were concerned would happen to them if they spoke up.) This was a big deal in the first century (v. 22). What results may you face for doing the same, if you unashamedly proclaim Christ?

The Pharisees did not exhibit teachable hearts. In this passage it is evident they go to great lengths to destroy the credibility of Christ. They would not submit or accept Christ's authority. Their pride inhibited their spiritual vision. Multiple times in the Gospels we see Jesus label the Pharisees as blind guides, blind fools, or blind men (Matthew 15:14; 23:16, 17, 24). Their strong-willed pride prevented them from accurately seeing and acknowledging Christ for who He was. Humbling themselves would have sabotaged their lives and all they had worked for. Such devastating results occur when we fail to get the "I" out of P-R-I-D-E.

The blind man acknowledged what the sighted could not see.

> *"Some thought they had no need of the enlightenment Jesus brought, because they could perfectly see well already, turned their backs on him and, without realizing it, moved into deeper darkness. Blame did attach to those who, while living in darkness, claimed to be able to see, like those religious leaders who were present and heard Jesus' pronouncement about the effect of his coming. To be so self-deceived as to shut one's eyes to the light is a desperate state to be in: the light is there, but if people refuse to avail themselves of it but rather deliberately reject it, how can they be enlightened? As Jesus said, their sin remains."* [3]

The revealing twist in John 9—the Pharisees were the blind ones. The man who was born blind actually acknowledged what the sighted could not see. His response was belief and worship of Jesus Christ, an appropriate acknowledgment for anyone whose spiritual vision is rightly restored.

God wants to bring precision to our vision. When we see clearly, others can clearly see Christ in us. He is our reference point and when we are not focused on Him we suffer the consequences of allowing our sight to be misguided.

Spiritual blindness prevents us from seeing the true condition of our hearts. This blindness will always cause us to question, doubt and discredit Jesus, which is a roadblock to a genuine relationship with Him. Questioning God's authority elevates ourselves to a position that doesn't belong to us. This act of rebellion will keep us spiritually blind until we bow before the Almighty.

God wants to bring precision to our vision.

In closing, spend some time reflecting on your spiritual vision. Ask the Lord to reveal any blindness He may want to give sight to and thank Him for His love that draws you to Him and His truth. Worship the beauty of Christ that results from accurate spiritual vision. God desires to restore clarity to a humble, contrite, teachable heart.

3 Ibid. p. 220-221.

Day 5: Just Like Jesus

The perfect example of Christ is sobering. In the entire history of our world, the ultimate act of humility was expressed by a man who bore the vile sin of every man, and was violently murdered though innocent. He adorned His body with a wreath of needles and three over-size nails then He reduced His life to two wooden boards. Christ's humility bought our delivery from the enormity of our depravity, and its consequences.

1. How did Jesus make Himself nothing? What was His life characterized by?

2. Jesus' example of a servant is a powerful charge to us. What risks/sacrifices will you need to make to be a servant like Christ?

Serving was Christ's demonstration of love to us. As a perfect example, Christ expressed how we, in turn, should serve others. His example of humility should motivate us to give up our lives for others, as an act of serving Him. Being a servant requires humility. Humility enforces our ability to serve others as Christ intended.

It's hard, friends. I get it. Serving like Christ requires supernatural strength because all too often our "me first" mindset likes to be catered to. It's especially difficult to serve challenging people, those we may feel are under serving, or undeserving. Until we include ourselves in the undeserving category, we will not fully realize the nature of our sin and unworthiness. Regardless of our job, position or influence . . . we are called to serve.

We have a choice: To serve selfishly or selflessly; to satisfy the temporal or the eternal. When we take our eyes off the eternal and focus on the temporal, our lives can appear daunting and repetitive. When we take our eyes off the temporal and focus on the eternal, our lives will look more like an example of Christ—a selfless servant.

Too easily we can focus on all we have to do instead of all the ministry God has given us. A shift in godly perspective teaches us that routine things in life and familiar faces should be viewed as blessings, not burdens; as ministry, not monotony. God gives us countless opportunities to serve: our families, co-workers, spouse, children, neighbors etc.

Matthew 20:26 reminds us that whoever wants to be great must become a servant. If we are to follow the example of Christ, Who did not come to be served, our mission must match His by serving others. *"Instead, whoever wants to become great among you must be your servant, and whoever wants to be first must be your slave—just as the Son of Man did not come to be served, but to serve, and to give his life as a ransom for many"* (Matthew 20:26-28). In God's kingdom, greatness = service.

The Greek words for serve (*diakoneō*) and servant (*diakonos*) come from the same root word, meaning to minister to another, to attend to anything that may serve another's interests, to provide or take care of the necessities of sustaining one's life. [1]

Later in this same section Jesus exhorts us by saying those who want to be first must be a slave. The Greek word for slave (*doulos*) means one who gives himself up for another's will, one whose service is used by Christ in advancing His cause among men and one who is devoted to another without regard to one's own interests. [2]

This is no easy task, friends. Jesus never said living like Him would come with comfort. But, this is His measure of greatness. The Pharisees sought greatness by living above others and reaching for accolades and advancement in the eyes of men. Remember what we learned earlier in the week; God opposes the proud but gives grace to the humble; those who exalt themselves will be humbled and those who humble themselves will be exalted. Do you see the connection? A truly humble servant will be exalted in the eyes of God, which is of far greater worth than being exalted in the eyes of men.

♡ Heart Exam

3. There are times when we may not feel like serving others. When physical strength appears limited or perhaps when others are ungrateful, this can rub us the wrong way. When do you find it hardest to serve others and who are the people you find it most difficult to serve?

4. Do you secretly want to be served? How does the desire for your service to be noticed cause you to serve selfishly?

The account of Jesus washing His disciple's feet in John 13:1-17, is another

1 http://classic.studylight.org/isb/view.cgi?number=1249 (accessed 3-19-2013).
2 http://classic.studylight.org/isb/view.cgi?number=1401 (accessed 3-19-2013).

Day 5

tender example for us to follow. Our Lord and King humbled Himself to serve His men by taking the lowliest position. In the first century, foot washing was a task given to servants as an act of hospitality to guests. Jesus served as an example to His inner twelve. He showed them exactly how they were to minister to others, by taking the position of a servant. John 13:14-15 says, *"Now that I, your Lord and Teacher, have washed your feet, you also should wash one another's feet. I have set you an example that you should do as I have done for you."*

5. In light of the instructions Paul gives us, how does humility play a role in displaying the attitude of Christ? What is one way you can model Jesus' example of humility this week?

Again we are challenged with putting others before ourselves. As stated in Day 1, "U" comes before "I" in H-U-M-I-L-I-T-Y. It's not a polite suggestion to be done whenever we feel like it. We are expected to exhibit Christlikeness and we do this best when the needs of others come before our own, when we resist selfishness and pride and consider others more important than self. Understand, there is a difference between properly taking care of ourselves to stay healthy, so we are able to serve others, than being self-absorbed.

In effect, as a servant of Christ, we are to give up our lives for the will of Christ in order to advance His kingdom. We are to minister to others by being devoted to serve their interests above our own. We cannot consider others better than ourselves, care about their interests or live unselfishly without lowering ourselves to a position of meekness.

Let's face it; we all have "those days." But we can't let the enemy and our own self-centered desires steal our joy and purpose for ministry, wherever God has us. We must remember to invest what is entrusted to us—to advance the Kingdom—to serve and not to be served.

Many of us may find ourselves right in the middle of privilege and entitlement, or pride and egotism. But Jesus came and implored a different life for us to follow. Wash feet. Give to the needy. Don't show favoritism. Be last. Give preference to others. Don't expect honor. Serve with a humble heart. Love the unlovely. Befriend the lowly. Forgive the difficult.

Day 5

6. How is following Jesus' example most difficult for you? What aspect of a Pharisaic life do you find the hardest to let go of?

Showing favoritism is the result of having an attitude for self, not Christ. When we regard some with special treatment over that of others, we're usually trying to position ourselves to get something in return, or to look as good as those we esteem. Yes, we should consider others more important and look to others' needs, but not to the exclusion of anyone else. We should treat others with equal fairness and love.

Read James 2:1-4 (Ponder what he says about favoritism.)

We are all guilty of showing favoritism. (Who we hang out with, who we sit by, who we reach out to, who we talk to and/or who we avoid, etc.) Or maybe we are tempted to act differently around those who may be well-known, popular, or those who hold significant titles, positions or degrees.

> *James 2:1-4*
>
> *[1]My brothers, as believers in our glorious Lord Jesus Christ, don't show favoritism. [2]Suppose a man comes into your meeting wearing a gold ring and fine clothes, and a poor man in shabby clothes also comes in. [3]If you show special attention to the man wearing fine clothes and say, "Here's a good seat for you," but say to the poor man, "You stand there" or "Sit on the floor by my feet," [4]have you not discriminated among yourselves and become judges with evil thoughts?*

7. How does favoritism reveal prejudice? What does this express about how we think of others?

If we're honest, we might admit there is probably a difference between how these *important people* are treated, from the unnoticed visitor at church, the disheveled looking woman at the grocery checkout, or the mother at the library who has unruly children. The connection favoritism plays in serving people is that we may tend to gravitate toward reaching out and serving those more *put together* than those who appear in need. This is symptomatic of a pharisaical heart because it seeks to serve those like themselves and pulls back from those who appear troubled *or* are just having a bad day.

Day 5

Truthfully, we are **all** in need. Christ can supernaturally enable us to view all people through His lens of equality regardless of people's appearance or status. Then, dispensing equal honor and respect to others will come more naturally as our spiritual vision obtains greater precision.

8. What impacts you the greatest from this week's lessons as a whole? How will you live differently as a result of what God has taught you this week?

Selfless serving is not selfish serving.

Selfless living characterizes a true servant of Christ. Selfless people think less often of themselves and more about the needs of others. When we serve others we are the hands and feet of Jesus. When we are selfless, we will serve with pure motives—to exude Jesus. If we are selfish, we will serve with ulterior motives—to be recognized or rewarded. Our purpose and desire should be to serve, just like Jesus. *"Serve wholeheartedly, as if you were serving the Lord, not men"* (Ephesians 6:7). *"If anyone serves, he should do it with the strength God provides, so that in all things God may be praised through Jesus Christ. To Him be the glory and the power for ever and ever. Amen"* (1 Peter 4:11b).

VIEWER GUIDE

John 13:1-17; Matthew 20:26

The ministry of the towel requires us to ____________ on ____________ strength.

The ministry of the towel is not __________________ .

The ministry of the towel is __________________________ .

1. _________ towels are Christ's tools for ministry.
2. _________ towels are His measure of biblical greatness.

Being the hands and feet of Jesus means letting others ____________________ Christ, through our love of them that stems from our love of _______ .

We need to grasp Who and why we serve. When we serve self, then we desire to ________ self so others will notice. When we serve Christ, our purpose is to _________ God and His kingdom, without considering what benefits us personally.

John 13:1-17 – Jesus stepped up to serve by _____________ to wash.

Greatness = Service. This kind of greatness comes from our ability to kneel and our _______________ to serve.

• •

Diakonos/Diakoneō – to minister to another, to attend to anything that may serve another's interests, to provide or take care of the necessities of sustaining one's life. [1]

Doulos – one who gives himself up for another's will, one whose service is used by Christ in advancing His cause among men and one who is devoted to another without regard to one's own interests. [2]

• •

Being a biblical servant is an attitude of the heart:

- † Whose heart removes _________ from the equation.
- † Whose choices satisfy the _____________ over the temporal.
- † Whose life characterizes Christ's example.
- † Whose purpose matches Christ's mission.
- † Whose ________________ is one of meekness and service.
- † Whose ________________ are to exalt and glorify God, not self.

The moment we accepted Christ we accepted the _________________ of the towel.

How _________ is your towel?

WEEK FIVE

Jesus' Wrongs Were Right

Day 1

Felony Fellowship

Day 2

Crimes In Customs

Day 3

Wrongful Worship & Rightful Reverence

Day 4

Sacrilegious Sabbath & Righteous Rest - part 1

Day 5

Sacrilegious Sabbath & Sinful Synagogue Service - part 2

WEEK FIVE—JESUS' WRONGS WERE RIGHT

Day 1: Felony Fellowship

I hope last week's lessons on pride and humility stretched and challenged not only our minds, but also our hearts. Reconciling the inevitable destruction of pride and welcoming the necessary characteristic of humility help us remain properly balanced in our relationship with God. Having a proper foundation of these two components will enable us to possess greater insight into the life of Christ and His teachings. Remember, when we are teachable, pride will not inhibit our discernment to the Lord's ways.

From a different angle, we will once again see some startling effects of pride and humility during our study this week. Our material will take a turn and focus on the life of Jesus and additional personal encounters He faced with the Pharisees and teachers of the Law. In the eyes of the Pharisees, Jesus was wrong on many levels. Repeatedly, we see their intent to prove His errors and slander His name. Jesus was growing in popularity and this agitated the Pharisees because they feared losing control of the people by having an individual rise above them. And, they were personally challenged by Christ's claims and all they held dear to their lives, especially the Law.

Whenever they interacted with Jesus He indiscriminately taught them truth, regardless of what they or others thought. Usually this meant they were the center of His teachings because of their faulty ways. As the spiritual leaders they could not welcome this man named Jesus educating *them* about the Law or other matters. Even though the Pharisees and teachers of the Law were wrong, they were blind to their sin. They continually insisted Christ was the wrong one.

This week we will address four specific perceived wrongs of Christ according to the Pharisees.

1. He hung out with all the wrong people.
2. He denounced the Pharisees' societal standards and customs.
3. He failed to lawfully observe the Sabbath.
4. He did not properly worship in the synagogue.

Ultimately, we will learn this week that Jesus' wrongs were undeniably right. His pattern for living should become ours if we are, according to the Pharisees, willing to have the same wrongs as Jesus.

Jesus is accused of enlisting the wrong disciples and fellowshipping with the wrong people. But, who exactly would the right people have been? The fact that the Pharisees established "wrong people" proves the judgment buried within their hearts by declaring certain individuals unworthy of friendship or fellowship. He clashed with the Pharisees' expectations. To be blunt, the wrong people Jesus rubbed shoulders with were sinners. Of course, the teachers of the Law would not associate themselves with such societal scum. Instead they separated themselves with the elite or other like-minded individuals.

Day 1

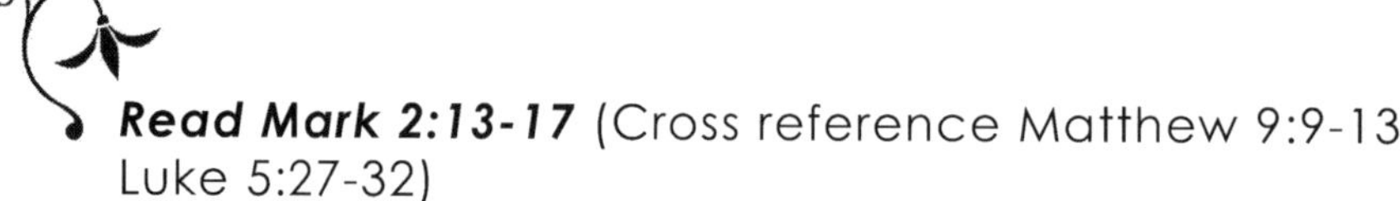

Read Mark 2:13-17 (Cross reference Matthew 9:9-13; Luke 5:27-32)

1. Describe the scenario Jesus is in. Is He condoning sin?

2. The final verse reveals a specific truth. Jesus shows the difference between those who are healthy and those who are sick. What does Jesus' statement reveal about spiritual transformation?

> *Matthew 9:9-13*
>
> *[9]As Jesus went on from there, he saw a man named Matthew sitting at the tax collector's booth. "Follow me," he told him, and Matthew got up and followed him. [10]While Jesus was having dinner at Matthew's house, many tax collectors and "sinners" came and ate with him and his disciples. [11]When the Pharisees saw this, they asked his disciples, "Why does your teacher eat with tax collectors and 'sinners'?" [12]On hearing this, Jesus said, "It is not the healthy who need a doctor, but the sick. [13]But go and learn what this means: 'I desire mercy, not sacrifice.' For I have not come to call the righteous, but sinners."*

Let's clarify a few things. First, Matthew is a tax collector. He assessed the value of goods and collected the taxes due to the Roman government. Based on Mark's account he must have handled the shipping and trade by the Sea of Galilee. Often times tax gatherers would increase the tax in order to add a little profit margin to their wallets. They had notorious reputations as licensed extortionists. Because Matthew belonged to a class of traitors that was excommunicated by fellow Jews, it was enough to make him despised, and his cooperation with the Romans further ostracized him from his own people. [1] For Jesus to invite such a person, with a tainted background, to be his disciple was beyond radical in the eyes of the religious leaders. This would be like asking a drug dealer to be the preacher of a church. Of course, I'm sure the Pharisees also wondered why they weren't chosen to be Christ's disciples. Surely they were more likely the type. Or were they?

Secondly, the scene is magnified when Matthew throws a big shin-dig at his house with all of his fellow tax buddies. This would be like bringing Las Vegas or the Red Light District to our living rooms. Here's the real shocker: Jesus joins them! Unbelievable!

In the first century when people were invited to a home it was more than ordinary hospitality. This held greater significance because of the value placed on what was called table fellowship. Jesus' reception of these people showed that He welcomed them into His life and was willing to associate with them. The Pharisees believed being with such people would defile them ceremonially. Jesus is teaching that He will bring sinners to repentance and forgiveness rather than being made unclean by association with them. [2] This message of salvation for sinners is the core of the gospel Jesus proclaimed.

---

1 *A Harmony of the Gospels by Robert L. Thomas & Stanley N. Gundry. Harper San Francisco Publishers, © 1978, p. 55.*

2 *ESV Study Bible Crossway Bibles. © 2008, p. 1960.*

Jesus left customary Jewish circles for those who were spiritually sick. Those who were confident in their own righteousness alienated themselves from Christ. The Pharisees thought they were spiritually healthy because of their strict adherence to the Law. As we learned last week they were actually blind to their spiritual depravity. The passage in Matthew 9:13 quotes Hosea 6:6 *"I desire mercy not sacrifice."* If they had true compassion, as God desired, they would have been compelled to care for others as Jesus did.

♡ *Heart Exam*

In the way you relate to "undesirables," are you more:

- like Matthew (invite them over)?
- like the Pharisees (look down on them)?
- like Jesus (become friends and offer the hope of Christ)?

3. What prejudices do you see evident in yourself, the church, culture and community where you live? (Class, wealth, education level, race, clothing or hair style, body piercing or tattoos, gender, physical appearance, location of living, etc.)

4. As you try to follow Jesus, are you loving others more freely, or becoming more constrained by religious rules? How so?

Until we acknowledge our need for Christ to spiritually transform us we will not receive Him nor invite Him into our lives. Instead, we'll replace true fellowship with Christ by elevating works and our confidence in them, while neglecting the practical needs of those around us. This was the demise of the religious leaders.

Later in the Gospels we see another narrative account of Christ in the company of more sinners. This encounter preludes three parables He uses to teach a specific lesson. As you read, notice the progression of each parable and the value placed on the item that is lost.

Day 1

Read Luke 15:1-32

The "sinners" gathered around to hear Christ talk while the Pharisees ridiculed His reception of such riffraff. Jesus responds with three powerful parables to drive home His point: Those who are lost need to be found, those who are spiritually dead need to be made spiritually alive and those who repent will be rejoiced over.

5. What do these parables reveal about Jesus' purpose in hanging out with sinners?

6. How often do you interact with unsaved people? Who do you have over for dinner, vacation with and do social outings with? Name the unsaved people you have visited with this past week.

7. Name those in your sphere of influence who are unreached for Christ or those you consider unacceptable? (Co-workers, neighbors, classmates, family, parents at soccer field, etc.) Specifically share how you can be more welcoming to them. How will you incorporate these ideas into your family life this week, month and permanently?

It's important to develop relationships with those God intersects our lives with. Please pause and pray for these people by name. Sincerely ask the Lord to open your heart to their need, to serve them and to exude, not exclude, God's love to them. Ask for courage to invite them into your life so they may see the glorious light of Christ and desire to possess this Light themselves.

Luke verse 2 says, *"And the Pharisees and the scribes grumbled, saying 'This man receives sinners and eats with them.'"* The Greek word for "grumble" (*diagogguzo*) means to murmur and is referenced as indignant complaining.[3] The word used for "receive" (*prosdechomai*) means to accept one into companionship and give access to one's self.[4] Interestingly, the word for "sinners" (*hamartolos*) is more an adjective than a noun. This word is describing one who is devoted to sin, and especially wicked, and can also refer to those who have specific vices or crimes, like those of tax collectors.[5]

The Pharisees were less than thrilled with Christ's choice of friends. Rather than reject these heathen individuals, Christ embraced them into His circle. Though viewed as outcasts by the religious leaders Christ saw them in need of spiritual healing, thus removing the barrier the Pharisees wanted to leave erected.

We will never meet an individual who does not matter deeply to God. We will never pay a grocery clerk Christ was not crucified for. We will never deposit a check with a banker Christ did not bleed for. We will never sit in an athletic arena with souls Christ did not suffer for. We will never have neighbors Christ was not nailed for. We will never play at a park with people Christ was not pierced for. We will never have our hair cut by a heart Christ did not hang for. We will never labor side-by-side with co-workers Christ was not wounded for.

We will never greet a fellow man Christ does not give grace to. We will never meet a mother Christ does not offer mercy to. We will never know a soccer family who Christ does not want to be a friend to. We will never rub shoulders with any human who Christ does not extend hope to. We will never see a father Christ does not grant forgiveness to. We will never make eye contact with anyone who is not equally loved by our Maker. Every individual matters to the Great I Am. How much do they matter to you?

---

3 http://classic.studylight.org/isb/view.cgi?number=1234 (accessed 3-26-2013).
4 http://classic.studylight.org/isb/view.cgi?number=4327 (accessed 3-26-2013).
5 http://classic.studylight.org/isb/view.cgi?number=268 (accessed 3-26-2013).

Day 2: Crimes In Customs

According to the religious leaders, Jesus picked the wrong disciples and congregated with the wrong kind of people. As mentioned yesterday, His willingness to mingle with such individuals heightened His misdemeanor meter in the eyes of the Pharisees and teachers of the Law. No sooner does Jesus declare the "rightness" of His association with sinners, His disciples commit a customary crime. Again, Jesus challenges some deeply held notions of the religious leaders.

Read Matthew 9:14-17 (Cross reference Mark 2:18-22; Luke 5:33-39)

Jesus is confronted with a question concerning fasting customs of the day. Before we dive into His response to His inquirers, we need to have a greater understanding of fasting in order to accurately comprehend Jesus' teaching. Fasting was to deny oneself of food and water for a period of time, typically from sun-up to sun-down. This custom was observed as a sign of mourning from sin, to ward off God's wrath and receive His compassion. Fasts were accompanied by humbling oneself with prayer and by wearing sackcloth as a symbol of penance and sorrow. [1]

According to the Law, Jews were required to fast only once a year, on the Day of Atonement. Let's rewind for a moment. During the Babylonian captivity there are other examples of fasting for sin, special occasions or impending disaster. After captivity there were four annual fasts held in commemoration of the national destruction the nation of Israel had overcome. Fasting was also commonly practiced when someone special died. Now, let's fast forward. During the early church, fasting, coupled with prayer, was practiced before the laying on of hands for teachers and elders (Acts 13:2-3; 14:23) and during times of tremendous difficulty (Acts 27:1-38). [2]

Even before the time of Christ the prophets warned against the abuse of fasting (Isaiah 58:3-7; Jeremiah 14:10-12; Zechariah 7, 8). The Israelites misunderstood its value being connected to purity of heart and a righteous life. The prophets taught that fasting was useless when it was separated from a life devoted to God.

Here we are now, addressing the time of Christ when the ritual of fasting was being misused and inappropriately expected. From the parable in Luke 18:12 we know that fasting twice a week may have been a common practice for these religious leaders. Earlier, in Matthew 6:16-18, Jesus teaches, *"And when you fast, do not look gloomy like the hypocrites, for they disfigure their faces that their fasting may be seen by others. Truly, I say to you, they have received their reward. But when you fast, anoint your head and wash your face that your fasting may not be seen by others but by your Father who is in secret. And your Father who sees in secret will reward you."*

---

1 Harper's Bible Dictionary by Paul J. Achtemeier. Harper San Francisco Publishers, © 1985, p. 304.
2 Pictorial Bible Dictionary by Merrill C. Tenney. Zondervan Publishing, © 1967, p. 278.

Day 2

The religious leaders made a public show of their fasting. Their appearance was depressing and their disfigured faces implied that instead of washing them perhaps they dusted their faces with ash.

They added their own man-made custom and elevated it to mandatory religious practice in an effort to appear extra spiritual *and* expected others to follow suit. Similar to the Pharisees questioning why Jesus' disciples didn't wash their hands before eating in Week Two, the real core question they are aiming at here is, *"Why don't your disciples fast like us?"* Jesus did not command or order His disciples to fast. The disciples actually weren't doing anything wrong by not fasting. What really irritated the Pharisees is the disciple's lack of compliance and agreement to their "man-made, law-adding" religious expectations.

Luke 18:12

12 I fast twice a week and give a tenth of all I get.

Heart Exam

1. How may you be conforming to man-made rituals? What Christian things do you do that you expect others to do? (Things that are extra-biblical.)

2. When does Jesus approve or disapprove of fasting? What is the key factor for fasting to be authentic?

3. If Christianity is not about conforming to man-made rules and welcoming the applause of external piety, then what is it about?

Day 2

The Pharisees wanted the spotlight on their super-sized sainthood. Their external piety received the attention they desired as red-carpet walkers. But, the internal purity is what Christ emphasized. In addition to fasting, giving alms and praying were the other two pillars of Jewish piety. Let's address these spiritual disciplines and how Jesus tied them to the appropriateness of what He is teaching.

In verse 1, Jesus warns that we are not to do "acts of righteousness" before men so that they are seen by them. When we do this we will fail to receive a reward from our Father in heaven.

4. Can you see any personal characteristics of a hypocrite in yourself from these passages?

5. Jesus teaches we are to give to those in need in secret. How does giving in secret help keep our hearts pure? Why are things done in secret rewarded by God?

6. Share a time when you have given "publicly" and a time when you gave "secretly." What gave you greater blessing?

Jewish public prayer was common morning, noon and night. During these set times they would set aside what they were doing to pray. Some did so discreetly while others did so candidly. Jesus is not objecting to public prayer, as we know even He prayed publicly (Matthew 14:19; 15:36). But, in this passage He is emphasizing a deeper truth regarding the condition of our hearts.

7. What greater value does private prayer invite? How should we pray?

We can't stand approved by God when we live spiritual lives for public acclaim. When we are tempted to gain approval for the external things we do, we are seeking to receive man's reward over God's. Our greater satisfaction should be to gain the applause and attention of God, by praying and giving in secret.

Jesus didn't approve of the Pharisees' self-serving supplications, frequent fasts or attention getting gifts. All of these practices are good things and should be properly experienced with a contrite heart—between us and the Lord. Sadly, self-righteousness exalts ego above even good things, thus extinguishing any heavenly reward and robbing self of true spiritual blessings. Insolence perpetually inhibits intimacy with Christ. The condition of our hearts will evermore be grounded in our intentions and the purity of our motives.

As we've seen today the Pharisees were ready to indict Jesus with a customs crime because of His disciples' lack of fasting. Jesus also challenged their assumptions with prayer and giving to those in need. The religious leaders were continually on guard to catch Jesus *or* His disciples doing anything that was contrary to their standards. The more evidence they could gather against Christ, the easier case they would have to convict Him guilty for breaking the Law and dispose Him from further interruption of their comfortable life of ease and self-glorification.

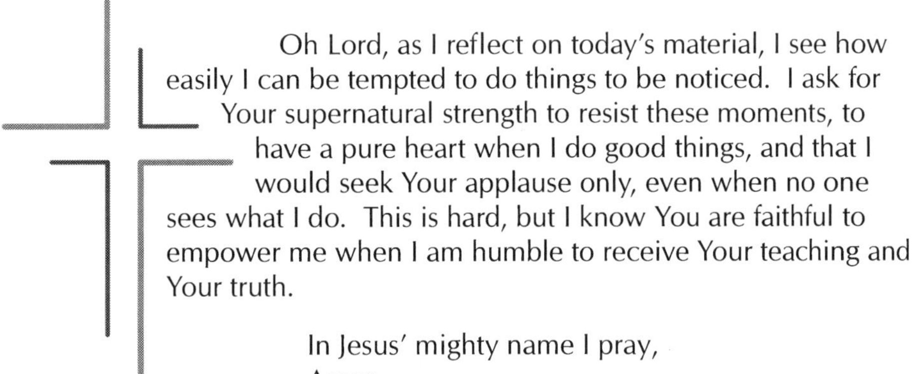

Oh Lord, as I reflect on today's material, I see how easily I can be tempted to do things to be noticed. I ask for Your supernatural strength to resist these moments, to have a pure heart when I do good things, and that I would seek Your applause only, even when no one sees what I do. This is hard, but I know You are faithful to empower me when I am humble to receive Your teaching and Your truth.

In Jesus' mighty name I pray,
Amen.

Day 3: Wrongful Worship & Rightful Reverence

Based on what we've gleaned thus far regarding fasting, this sets the stage for Jesus' response to the Pharisees' question in Matthew 9:14-17: *"Why do John's disciples and the disciples of the Pharisees fast, but your disciples do not fast?"* The Pharisees deemed the disciples wrong for not fasting.

Re-read Matthew 9:14-17 (Cross reference Mark 2:18-22; Luke 5:33-39)

> *John 7:39*
>
> *[39]By this he meant the Spirit, whom those who believed in him were later to receive. Up to that time the Spirit had not been given, since Jesus had not yet been glorified.*

Jesus tells them why. The solemnity of fasting would be incongruent to the elation they should be experiencing since the Bridegroom, Jesus, has arrived. His presence ushered in the Kingdom of God and was cause for celebration and joy. The Pharisees religion lacked jubilation and cheer. They appeared mournful through their fasting. Our joy comes from the confident presence of Christ in our lives. Jesus is teaching that our faith should be expressed more like a wedding than a funeral. When Jesus is taken away for good, His disciples will fast; but then fasting will be an appropriate response with the occasion of His death.

Rather than mending and covering up customary practices of righteousness within Jewish tradition, Jesus is offering real growth in heavenly righteousness, which He compares to new wine in new wineskins. [1] Jesus brings refreshment and new expressions of faith. We can't confine our new life in Christ to the old observances and customs.

> *"Jesus is describing the nature of a new relationship He came to bring. For centuries, the Jews worshiped in the temple, practicing solemn rituals. He was bringing a new type of worship with vitality, warmth and intimacy that could be expressed with gladness, joy and celebration. Sometimes we lose sight of this. Church services today are often borrowed from an Old Testament concept of solemn, ritualized worship—but this is not the image of worship presented by Jesus. Worship is a feast, not a fast. It is a time of celebration, not solemnity. In Christ, we have a living, dynamic relationship. We must not contain it in old structures, old forms, old rituals, old ideas and old attitudes. The new system (our relationship with Christ) has come. It is too powerful and will destroy the old forms that try to contain it."* [2]

Heart Exam

1. Describe your worship and relationship with God. Is it more like a wedding or funeral? How does the newness of joy inspire you to deeper reverence and adoration of God?

---

1 *ESV Study Bible Crossway Bibles. © 2008, p. 1837.*

2 *Marveling With Mark by Steven A. Crane. Wipf & Stock, © 2010, p. 49.*

2. Share an example of an old form(s) you have broken free from? Despite any fears you may have experienced how did this change produce positive results in your heart and worship of Christ?

Any style or method of worship can become rote, ritualized and mundane. Jesus addressed what was typical of His day. But even 2,000 years later as followers of the new era, we can still experience the same stale and stiff worship that was present in the first century and fail to sincerely honor God.

When Jesus encounters the Samaritan woman at the well in John 4:19-24, He tells her worship of God will no longer be limited to the temple in Jerusalem. Jesus brings a new meaning to worship which is evidenced by His proclamation that genuine worship will not be bound by a geographical location any longer. *"Yet a time is coming and has now come when the true worshipers will worship the Father in spirit and truth, for they are the kind of worshipers the Father seeks. God is Spirit, and his worshipers must worship in spirit and in truth"* (John 4:23-24).

"God is spirit" means that God is not made up of physical matter, but is rather omnipresent; His existence is present everywhere. Until the time of Christ worshipers went to the tabernacle (and later the temple) to worship God through rituals and regulations (Hebrews 9:1). But Jesus inaugurated a new ability to worship God anywhere because of His indwelling Holy Spirit. After Christ's death the Spirit of God moved from a building to each believer's body (John 7:39). Christ followers become the temple of God (1 Corinthians 3:16-17; 6:19; Ephesians 2:19-22) and, therefore, they can now worship God in any place because of His divine presence within them.

The time had arrived, and the old forms were being replaced with new ways, and through Jesus, a new nature for worship was instituted.

> *"Christians shall worship God, not in the ceremonial observances of the Mosaic institution, but in spiritual ordinances, consisting less in bodily exercise, and animated and invigorated more with divine power and energy. The way of worship which Christ has instituted is rational and intellectual, and refined from those external rites and ceremonies with which the Old-Testament worship was both clouded and clogged."* [3]

Authentic worship of God is not contained to a place or building. The real question is not "where" but rather "how" one will worship. We should be concerned not only in the object of our worship (God), but also in the manner in which we worship Him. His worshipers must worship in spirit and in truth.

1 Corinthians 3:16-17

[16]Don't you know that you yourselves are God's temple and that God's Spirit lives in you? [17]If anyone destroys God's temple, God will destroy him; for God's temple is sacred, and you are that temple.

1 Corinthians 6:19

[19]Do you not know that your body is a temple of the Holy Spirit, who is in you, whom you have received from God? You are not your own;

Ephesians 2:22

[22]And in him you too are being built together to become a dwelling in which God lives by his Spirit.

3 *Matthew Henry Commentary http://www.blueletterbible.org/commentaries/comm_view.cfm?AuthorID=4&contentID=1670&commInfo=5&topic=John (accessed 3-28-2013).*

Day 3

> *"Sincere heart devotion, whenever and wherever found, is indispensable if men and women would present to God worship which he can accept. The worship in which he takes delight is accordingly spiritual worship – the sacrifice of a humble, contrite, grateful and adoring spirit."* [4]

Believers are to worship God in the Spirit by the truth of Who Christ is. Many discrepancies arose concerning Christ, His purpose and mission. False claims were made that rejected His authority. The transliterated Greek word used here for truth in John 4:24 is (*aletheia*). Its definition is, *"the truth as taught in the Christian religion, respecting God and the execution of his purposes through Christ, and respecting the duties of man, opposing alike to the superstitions of the Gentiles and the inventions of the Jews, and the corrupt opinions and precepts of false teachers even among Christians."* [5] Possessing accurate truth of Christ and God is necessary for our worship to be genuine. Otherwise, we may as well worship Superman. There are undeniable doctrinal truths to be sincerely accepted within our hearts.

3. Based on what you've learned today, what is the difference between wrongful worship and rightful reverence? Share a time when you may have experienced either one.

4. We need to consider the impact the indwelling Holy Spirit makes in our worship and relationship with God. How does this truth bring greater freedom to your worship? What do you struggle to grasp?

5. How do you worship God whenever and wherever? Is your worship more of a lifestyle or a liturgy?

4 The Gospel of John by F.F. Bruce. William B. Eerdmans Publishing, © 1983, p. 111.
5 http://www.blueletterbible.org/lang/lexicon/lexicon.cfm?Strongs=G225&t=KJV (accessed 3-28-2013).

6. What have you gained the most about this subject matter of worshiping God in spirit and in truth? If you have viewed worship as merely corporate worship on Sunday mornings, what needs to change for you to move past this inaccurate understanding?

What the Pharisees considered wrong, Jesus declared right. The Pharisees worship was counterfeit at worst, and carnal at best. Even in the Old Testament God desired a contrite heart. But oftentimes people were caught up in the external displays. Jesus ushered in a new and intimate change for worship. And true to His nature, He will distinguish true worshipers from hypocrites.

Hopefully we've learned today that true worship does not merely exist in brick and mortar once a week from 10:00-11:30 a.m. No. If we relegate worship to a certain day each week or to just singing songs, we miss its true meaning and mission. In fact, many people can go to church and not even truly worship God. Worship is an attitude and expression of our hearts, residing and exuding from within the temple of the Holy Spirit. Our greatest expression of worship will result from our deepest connection to His love. ***"Therefore, since we are receiving a kingdom that cannot be shaken, let us be thankful, and so worship God acceptably with reverence and awe"*** (Hebrews 12:28).

Spend some time privately worshiping God. Excuse yourself from a noisy house. Or perhaps drive to a place where you can quiet your heart from any distractions and your focus can be stilled in His presence. Use the space below to share anything He may stir within you.

Day 4: Sacrilegious Sabbath & Righteous Rest — part 1

While Jesus' actions on Day 2 may have warranted a misdemeanor, His choices in today's lesson will reveal a paramount felony in the eyes of the first-century Jewish leaders. The Pharisees frequently charged Jesus with breaking the Sabbath according to the Mosaic Law. This sacrilegious offense outraged the Pharisees and teachers of the Law because they were the experts in all matters pertaining to the Law and knew the penalty due for blasphemy. Jesus forces them to re-evaluate their faulty presuppositions.

The Hebrew word for Sabbath (*shabbath*) means a rest or ceasing from work. God inaugurated the Sabbath at creation (Genesis 1:1-2:3). He rested from all His work on the seventh day. He also blessed the Sabbath and set it apart as holy. Specific mention of the Sabbath occurs later in Exodus 16:21-30, where the Israelites were to gather a double portion of manna on the sixth day, in order to rest on the seventh.

Shortly after, Moses delivered the Ten Commandments (Exodus 20). Verses 8-11 announce the fourth commandment: *"Remember the Sabbath day by keeping it holy."* The Israelites were instructed to commemorate the Sabbath weekly and not labor. Nor were their children, servants or animals to work. Severe punishment ensued for those who violated this covenant (Exodus 31:14-17; 35:1-3; Numbers 15:32-36).

Sabbath observance was a cornerstone to the Israelites' faith and religious practice. God intended for this day to be a blessing and joy to the Jews, physically and spiritually. It was not only a day of rest but also one for worship of Yahweh. Later in Deuteronomy 5:15, Moses also commanded the Israelites to keep the Sabbath as remembrance of God's deliverance from their bondage in Egypt.

> *With the development of the synagogue during the Exile, the Sabbath became a day for worship and the study of the Law, as well as a day of rest. During the period between Ezra and the Christian era the scribes formulated innumerable legal restrictions for the conduct of life under the law. Two whole treatises in the Talmud are devoted to the details of Sabbath observance.* [1]

These imposed restrictions by the scribes were extra-biblical regulations. Jesus is exceedingly critical of these mandates, as they are the basis for many of the conflicts He faced with the religious leaders and experts of the Law. In Luke 11:46, Jesus warns these individuals, *"And you experts in the law, woe to you, because you load people down with burdens they can hardly carry, and you yourselves will not lift one finger to help them."*

In essence, they established a law around the Law by adding provisions that were never advised, but were enforced as mandatory to abide by. The additional rules and traditions were cumbersome to follow.

---

1 *NIV Compact Dictionary of the Bible by J.D. Douglas & Merrill C. Tenney. Zondervan Publishing House, © 1989. p. 514.*

Day 4

Many of the early Christians in the New Testament were Jews who continued to keep the Sabbath. Because the resurrection was central to their faith they began to meet for worship on the first day of the week and designated it as the Lord's Day (Matthew 28:1; Acts 2:1; 1 Corinthians 16:2).

Our passage for study today is necessary to accurately comprehend the purpose and intent of the Sabbath. Jesus doesn't question Sabbath Law, rather He debunks the religious leaders' assumptions, and tests their expert authority and interpretation of the Law.

Read Matthew 12:1-14 (Cross reference Mark 2:23-28; 3:1-6; Luke 6:1-11)

Because of their additional man-made traditions, the Pharisees equated "picking grain" to the works of reaping, threshing and winnowing.

1. What does Leviticus 19:9-10; 23:22, teach, and how does this reveal God's compassion to the needy?

Jesus vindicates Himself and His disciples with four biblical examples. Let's review them one at a time.

Read Leviticus 24:5-9

2. The first example Jesus uses is King David. If Scripture does not convict or punish David for eating the bread of the Presence; what does this disclose about the intent of the Law? What does Mark 2:27 say?

3. Jesus' second example is with the priests. Jesus says the priests "profaned" the Sabbath, yet were also innocent. Is this contradictory or are there allowances made within the Law? Who has the authority to do this?

Luke 6:1-11

1 One Sabbath Jesus was going through the grain fields, and his disciples began to pick some heads of grain, rub them in their hands and eat the kernels.
2 Some of the Pharisees asked, "Why are you doing what is unlawful on the Sabbath?"
3 Jesus answered them, "Have you never read what David did when he and his companions were hungry?
4 He entered the house of God, and taking the consecrated bread, he ate what is lawful only for priests to eat. And he also gave some to his companions."
5 Then Jesus said to them, "The Son of Man is Lord of the Sabbath."
6 On another Sabbath he went into the synagogue and was teaching, and a man was there whose right hand was shriveled.
7 The Pharisees and the teachers of the law were looking for a reason to accuse Jesus, so they watched him closely to see if he would heal on the Sabbath.
8 But Jesus knew what they were thinking and said to the man with the shriveled hand, "Get up and stand in front of everyone." So he got up and stood there.
9 Then Jesus said to them, "I ask you, which is lawful on the Sabbath: to do good or to do evil, to save life or to destroy it?"
10 He looked around at them all, and then said to the man, "Stretch out your hand." He did so, and his hand was completely restored.
11 But they were furious and began to discuss with one another what they might do to Jesus.

Day 4

4. Matthew 12:6, 8, communicates the third biblical example Christ used to exonerate Himself. Who is the "one greater" and how does verse 8 reinforce this?

5. How does Matthew 12:7 challenge the Pharisees? What is Jesus trying to teach them? Who is really guilty of breaking the Sabbath, and why?

6. How have you questioned or convicted someone of sacrilegious Sabbath observance? Have you been judged by how you spent your day of rest? (We'll go more in depth in Day 5, but please share an example here.)

Jesus rebuts the religious leaders' accusations. The Pharisees played with an extra deck of cards, stacked high with multiple Sabbath exclusions that were not intended.

> *"One of the treatises in the Talmud enumerates thirty-nine principal classes of prohibited actions. Each of these chief enactments was further discussed and elaborated, so that actually there were several hundred things a conscientious, law-abiding Jew could not do on the Sabbath."* [2]

The Pharisees perception was convoluted, compared to the actual intent of the Law regarding Sabbath observance. The Law extended mercy to those in need. And, as Jesus claims, the Sabbath's purpose was to serve God's people, not the other way around. Once again, the Pharisees' practice of religious rituals trumped weightier matters of compassion. Had they truly understood Hosea 6:6 they would have kept quiet—and perhaps even helped to feed these hungry disciples.

Hosea 6:6

[6]For I desire mercy, not sacrifice, and acknowledgement of God rather than burnt offerings.

Jesus makes a bold declaration when He states in Matthew 12:8, ***"For the Son of Man is Lord of the Sabbath."*** Jesus claims to have the authority to interpret the Law. (There is more to come on Jesus' authority in Week Six.) The Sabbath pointed to Christ and the rest He came to bring. The first-century leaders were misguided in the actual necessities for salvation based from Scripture. Their extra-biblical requirements of "good works," for Sabbath and Law-keeping, were impossible for anyone to follow.

---

2 *Pictorial Bible Dictionary by Merrill C. Tenney. Zondervan Publishing House, ©1967. p. 736.*

The passage in Matthew 12 will hold more significance if we also glean Christ's teaching in the prior three verses of Matthew 11:28-30. This section provides an invitation to everyone who is tired and exhausted. Jesus gives an instruction for those who are overloaded by life and worn out by living. He simply says, *"Come to me, all you who are weary and burdened, and I will give you rest. Take my yoke upon you and learn from me, for I am gentle and humble in heart, and you will find rest for your souls. For my yoke is easy and my burden is light."* The souls of those in the first century were in desperate need of this kind of righteous rest.

The people Jesus addressed in this passage were oppressed and weighed down by the choking yoke of religious legalism, imposed by the Pharisees. The people experienced tremendous guilt for not being able to keep the Law, and all the additional stipulations. Their yoke kept getting heavier and more unbearable. Jesus tells them to put their neck under His yoke—His teaching—and follow Him. His burden is light, not heavy or troublesome unlike the religious leaders.'

♡ *Heart Exam*

7. Is there any religious legalism you may still be in bondage to? What steps will you take to break free?

8. How do you need to experience the kind of righteous rest Jesus offers?

9. Share a time when you allowed an extra-biblical tradition or obligation to overload you. How did you spiritually grow when you released yourself?

Jesus' invitation delivered refreshment and freedom to the people. They were learning that when they truly came to Him as this passage proposes; they recognized their soul was created for intimacy with the Father, not the load others placed on them. They could rest in His presence and not be encumbered by performance or religious obligation. The same is true for us. Come to Him . . . and rest.

Day 5: Sacrilegious Sabbath & Sinful Synagogue Service – part 2

Luke 13:10-17

*10 On a Sabbath Jesus
was teaching in one of
the synagogues, 11 and a
woman was there who
had been crippled by a
spirit for eighteen years.
She was bent over and
could not straighten
up at all. 12 When Jesus
saw her, he called
her forward and said
to her, "Woman, you
are set free from your
infirmity." 13 Then he
put his hands on her,
and immediately she
straightened up and
praised God. 14 Indignant
because Jesus had
healed on the Sabbath,
the synagogue leader
said to the people,
"There are six days for
work. So come and be
healed on those days,
not on the Sabbath."
15 The Lord answered
him, "You hypocrites!
Doesn't each of you on
the Sabbath untie your
ox or donkey from the
stall and lead it out to
give it water? 16 Then
should not this woman,
a daughter of Abraham,
whom Satan has kept
bound for eighteen
long years, be set free
on the Sabbath day
from what bound her?"
17 When he said this,
all his opponents were
humiliated, but the
people were delighted
with all the wonderful
things he was doing.*

John 7:21-24

*21 Jesus said to them,
"I did one miracle, and
you are all astonished.
22 Yet, because Moses
gave you circumcision
(though actually it
did not come from
Moses, but from
the patriarchs), you
circumcise a child on
the Sabbath. 23 Now if a
child can be circumcised
on the Sabbath so that
the law of Moses may
not be broken, why
are you angry with me
for healing the whole
man on the Sabbath?
24 Stop judging by mere
appearances, and make
a right judgment."*

Shortly after Jesus' encounter in the grain fields with His disciples and the Pharisees, He entered the local synagogue. After setting the Pharisees straight on Sabbath strictness and biblical grace, He is now confronted with a disabled man's hand. Would Jesus heal him? After all, it was the Sabbath. He knew the religious leaders were closely watching His every move. They were hoping for an opportunity to accuse Him as a law-breaker.

The Pharisees knew the letter of the Law, but failed to exhibit the spirit of the law, which is what Jesus did. He released captives from bondage and extended grace and freedom to their spiritual lives. He did the good He knew He ought to do, regardless of what day it was or what tradition prevented.

Read Matthew 12:9-14; Mark 3:1-6; Luke 6:6-11 (Please read all three. Each account provides new insight to the others.)

Heart Exam

1. What does Jesus' question in Matthew 12 reveal about the Pharisees' Sabbath conduct? How is Jesus' response a rebuke for these religious leaders?

Read Luke 13:10-17 (in the margin)

2. Add any similarities or additional insights about Sabbath healing and Jesus' response to naysayers.

Read John 7:21-24 (in the margin)

Day 5

3. What is Christ trying to teach in verse 24? Why were the Jews wrong? Add any more pertinent thoughts from Christ about the Sabbath.

4. How might your life exhibit double-standards? For example, when have you expected one thing of others, but were unwilling to abide yourself? Or have you bent the rules when it conveniently suited you?

Mark 3:4-5

[4]Then Jesus asked them, "Which is lawful on the Sabbath: to do good or to do evil, to save life or to kill?" But they remained silent. [5]He looked around at them in anger and, deeply distressed at their stubborn hearts, said to the man, "Stretch out your hand." He stretched it out, and his hand was completely restored.

Jesus asks another question in both Mark and Luke where the answer seems pretty obvious; but in Mark 3:4, the Pharisees remained silent. Their silence communicated their failure to truly understand the difference between what is sacred and what is sacrilege. In Mark 3:5, Jesus expresses deep distress and anger over the hardness of their hearts. This condition will prevent anyone from receiving Christ's teaching. Unless our stubbornness is relinquished and we allow Jesus' example to soften our hearts, we will never experience what He intended for the Sabbath.

Notice that both parties in Mark and Luke experienced anger and rage, but Jesus was justified in His. It's important to understand the difference between righteous indignation and unrighteous anger. Luke 6:8 says Jesus knew their thoughts. Even still, He fearlessly proceeded to heal the man's hand. In doing this Jesus declares it is lawful to do good on the Sabbath.

Luke 6:8-9

[8]But Jesus knew what they were thinking and said to the man with the shriveled hand, "Get up and stand in front of everyone." So he got up and stood there. [9]Then Jesus said to them, "I ask you, which is lawful on the Sabbath: to do good or to do evil, to save life or to destroy it?"

5. How might we get so closed minded that we fail to see and promote matters of grace and compassion within our community and church—regardless of what day of the week it may be? Be specific and think practically. For example, how would it be accepted to have a baby shower for an un-wed pregnant mother? Or, what would your church leaders think if you gave your tithe to a family in need instead of the church? What else could be relevant to your community or sphere of influence, but prohibited as an "unwritten" rule?

Day 5

When our hearts are hard and stubborn, Jesus is grieved, just like He was towards the Pharisees and teachers of the Law. They couldn't see past themselves or their misappropriated understanding. They neglected concerns of the heart and failed to promote grace, compassion and mercy. Jesus went toe-to-toe with them by emphatically announcing it was indeed lawful to do good and save a life on the Sabbath—without being disobedient to the Law. Their reaction to Christ's claims proves their continual unwillingness to hear and accept the truth.

6. With this in mind, how does this change your preconceived thoughts regarding the Sabbath day? Also, if the Sabbath is made for man, what is the biblical intent for Sabbath rest?

7. What Sunday restrictions did you have growing up? Do you still honor any of them? Does it have to be Saturday?

We are to love others as Christ loved us. Religious legalism barricades authentic Christianity and promotes counterfeit faith. We will fail to meet others' needs and be prompt to convict them of wrong when we live in a spiritual straight-jacket. Genuine love authenticates our faith because it is the way of Christ. His love triumphs over legalism.

Jesus challenged the Pharisees' and religious leaders' understanding of the Law. Their interpretation excluded sinners (Day 1), exalted religious performance with fasting (Day 2), encouraged mournful worship (Day 3), left people hungry (Day 4), and also left disabled individuals maimed (Day 5). In each account, Christ affirms His position and teaches truth.

> *"The Pharisees' attempt to keep the law and build a hedge around it, actually prevented them from the intent of the original Law. It is so easy to do. In fact, it is a danger of any movement. We make our own points of emphasis, we create our own ways of doing things, and we develop ritual. We take what is important to us and we put a hedge around it—and those things then determine for us what it means to be a Christian. The unspoken laws, the prescribed worship, the proper form create for us our own form of orthodoxy. The question is, are our rules what are important to God?*
>
> *"Think for a moment about all the traditions of Christianity that have become stale, stagnant and ritualistic. Ponder all the proper forms and ways of doing things that have become more important than substance. When this happens, the ritual itself becomes more important than*

> *compassion; and history and precedent become more important than purpose. No movement is exempt. Neither the one steeped in old stale tradition, nor the one opposed to tradition for whom opposing tradition becomes their practice."* [1]

In the eyes of the Pharisees, Jesus was wrong on many levels. His societal standards were others-centered, not tradition based. His friends and disciples were law-breakers, not staunch Law keepers. His ministry met people's needs, not personal greeds. His Sabbath observance was anti-legalistic, yet pro-love. Ultimately, His methods were non-conforming, yet His mission was transforming. Jesus' perceived wrongs were undeniably right. How willing are we to embrace Christ's ways and "rightly live wrongly?"

Lord Jesus, I have so much to consider from all I have learned this week regarding how rightly You lived despite the perceived wrongs by the Pharisees. Help me be motivated to deeper faith by Your example. Direct my thoughts to ponder those difficult heart questions that have caused me to search within and seek the Holy Spirit's guidance for right living. I ask in faith for You to make me courageous and intentional to rub shoulders with those who don't know You and I humbly seek Your forgiveness when my worship has been half-hearted. I need You, Jesus, to purify my heart.

In Your mighty name I pray,
Amen.

1 *Marveling With Mark by Steven A. Crane. Wipf & Stock, © 2010. p. 52-53.*

Mark 12:28-34; Deuteronomy 6:5; Mark 12:31; 1 John 4:7-12; John 13:35

Christ's love compels us; it compels us to do what is __________ even when others might see it as wrong. His love begins to change us from the inside out.

1. Worship is the result of our ________________ . Genuine worship of God is a ______________, not bound to a building once a week.

Worship is not about feeling good, being gratified or entertained. Worship is about ________ !

2. Worship invites _____________ . A heart seeking intimacy will reject ___________ .

How we love God is ________________ by how we worship Him.

3. Worship _____________ with __________ . "Love [1] the Lord your God with all [2] . . . "

- † Heart – denotes the center of all spiritual and physical life. The seat of our thoughts, passions, desires, appetites and affections.
- † Soul – the seat of the feelings and affections. It is the immaterial part of a person's being.
- † Mind – the faculty of understanding, reasoning, feeling, desiring, thinking.
- † Strength – ability, force, strength, might. How a person uses the abilities **they have**.

How we love God will ______________ how we love others. We cannot love others the way God ______________ until we love Him the way He ________________ .

"By this all men will know that you are my disciples, by how you__________ one another. "

4. Worship impacts our _____________ . People are a ________________ to Christ. They should be for us too.

Every individual _______________ to the Great I Am.

WEEK SIX

Pharisee or Follower?

Day 1

Christ's Authority

Day 2

A Follower's Responsibility

Day 3

Woes & Warnings

Day 4

Practice What You Preach

Day 5

Internal and External Purity

WEEK SIX—PHARISEE OR FOLLOWER?

Day 1: Christ's Authority

It's hard to believe this is our final week. What a wonderful journey we've explored together. As we wrap up our last week, I hope to reinforce the necessity of being constantly on guard to ensure our hearts are rightly aligned with God. Remember, from the beginning, whenever our hearts are out of sync with God, it affects all other areas of our lives. Repelling external piety, and instead, embracing internal purity, will help assure our hearts remain in proper agreement with the Lord and His will.

As we've studied encounters with the Pharisees, we would be remiss to assume we cannot identify with them. Some of their issues may not be presently pertinent to our lives, but I'm confident some aspect resonates within our souls, or may poke our consciences sometime later. This material is not a 12-step program and **boom** we are healed from a hypocritical life! This study is a call to action. Pharisaical tendencies will continue to sprout like unwanted weeds and may vary day-to-day. Being aware of these pitfalls is only part of the solution. Awareness is an important first step, but can be like gathering information. Information without transformation and application is useless. When we become aware of glaring weaknesses we need to respond accordingly. Applying biblical truth to what we know transforms our lives; and sanctification is a life-long transformative process.

We need to recognize and take to heart the severe rebuke Jesus reserved for this class of religious leaders. His harshest words were communicated to these pious pretenders and fraudulent fakers. Jesus made it very clear, the kingdom would not welcome such people. We must also be on guard to protect our hearts from their hypocrisy. He reminds us in Matthew 5:20, *"For I tell you that unless your righteousness surpasses that of the Pharisees and the teachers of the law, you will certainly not enter the kingdom of heaven."*

We've looked at how utterly wrong their lives were and it's easy to point a finger at them, but we are often just as guilty. Christ did not hesitate to teach the religious leaders accurate truth, and to correct their external piety and self-righteousness. He wants to do the same with us. Will we respond as they did by raising our noses and barricading our ears and hearts by rejecting Christ's authority? It's time to stop playing church. It's time to repent and humble our hypocritical hearts, purge piety and replace it with pure devotion to Christ.

As we wrap up this study, our final lessons will address a few more relevant issues in the lives of the Pharisees and teachers of the Law. Ultimately, we need to answer a critical question. Will we live the life of a Pharisee or the life of a follower of Christ Jesus? As we've learned, there are stark contrasts between the two. They are incongruent *and* not compatible: Legalism versus grace; hypocrisy versus authenticity; and external piety versus internal purity, to name a few.

The Pharisees had many issues with Jesus. Their biggest qualm though, was their resistance towards the validity of Christ's authority (Luke 20:1-2). He claimed to be greater than Abraham and the prophets, and eventually, Christ equated Himself to God (John 10:30-33; 8:58). Because of His authority and position, on

Day 1

multiple occasions He granted forgiveness of sin to individuals. This infuriated the religious leaders because only God can forgive sin and they believed Jesus blasphemed against God (Luke 7:49; Matthew 9:6; Mark 2:5-11). Many times the leaders tried to plot how they would kill this man named Jesus. Besides, who wants to hang around a guy who continually confronts our sin anyway?

> *"The Pharisees were at least theoretically against hypocrisy (if only they could see it). Their real quarrel was much deeper: they would have nothing to do with the personal claims of Jesus and the centrality of these claims to his message. Jesus, in fact, put his own person in that central place previously held by the Torah as God's revelation to his people."* [1]

John 8:58

58 "Very truly I tell you," Jesus answered, "before Abraham was born, I am!"

Heart Exam

Accepting Christ's authority in our lives is necessary. Of course, the initial acceptance of Him as Lord and Savior is foremost. But what about those difficult life choices we face and the tough daily decisions where we wrestle to submit? (Guarding our tongues, nurturing our families, honoring and respecting our husbands, wise or frivolous use of money and time, move or stay, resign or accept new job offer, etc.)

Luke 7:49

49 The other guests began to say among themselves, "Who is this who even forgives sins?"

1. When you choose your desires over God's will, what results have you experienced?

Luke 19:10 says, *"For the Son of Man came to seek and to save what was lost."* Matthew 9:12-13 also reveals Christ's purpose and mission. *"On hearing this, Jesus said, It is not the healthy who need a doctor, but the sick. But go and learn what this means: 'I desire mercy, not sacrifice.' For I have not come to call the righteous, but sinners.' "*

2. The Jews didn't believe Jesus was the Christ because they were not His sheep. How well do the attributes of being one of His sheep exist in your life?

1 *The Zondervan Encyclopedia of the Bible, Vol 4. Merrill C. Tenney, General Editor, Zondervan, Grand Rapids, MI @2009, p. 842-852.*

3. In order to prove His authority, what does Jesus refer to in verse 34? What does Jesus propose to these individuals?

The Pharisees knew the Torah and knew the Messiah was coming. He was the answer to their freedom—their ticket to overthrow the Romans. But their personal view of what the Anointed One would be like was far different from the reality of who Christ was. I imagine they expected someone a lot like them. They wanted one who thought the same, dressed the same, taught the same, judged the same and executed the Law the same as they. As we know, Jesus rocked their comfort boat and unsettled their righteous stride. Christ certainly did bring freedom to all and He did overthrow and crush Satan at the cross. But this isn't what the Pharisees sought. They rejected Christ's leadership because ultimately, He overthrew their pious lives.

> *"The Jews were convinced that when the long-awaited Messiah came, he would free the people from political oppression. He would liberate them from the power of the Roman Empire. They were looking for an earthly king to bring their nation into power. But Jesus' purpose was much deeper, his intentions more significant, and his kingship infinitely more glorious than what the people were expecting. They had to learn the true meaning of the 'Messiah'—Anointed One. They had to discover who Jesus really was. Only then would they have his okay to spread the Good News."* [2]

Matthew 16:1

[1]The Pharisees and Sadducees came to Jesus and tested him by asking him to show them a sign from heaven.

The religious leaders sought a special sign from Jesus to prove He was the Messiah. He had already performed numerous miracles, yet they wanted more (Matthew 16:1; Mark 8:11). Jesus wasn't performing for a circus; He was positioning Himself as the Savior. He didn't come to play tricks, He came to acquire trust. He is a King, not a clown. He came to bring glory to His Father. They had all the evidence they needed; they just plain rejected the truth the Messiah was in their midst. Jesus opposed their request for miracles and stated they would only receive the sign of Jonah.

Mark 8:11

[11]The Pharisees came and began to question Jesus. To test him, they asked him for a sign from heaven.

Read Matthew 12:38-42; 16:1-4

4. What was the sign of Jonah? (If you are unfamiliar with this story, take a moment to read the four short chapters of this book.) What did Jonah foreshadow?

2 *The Story. Zondervan Publishing, © 2008. p. 275.*

Day 1

5. Why will their generation be condemned? Also reference John 3:18. (The answer is two-fold.) Share how this may also apply to our generation personally.

6. Contrast the Ninevites' response to Jonah's preaching and the religious leader's response to Jesus' preaching.

Ninevites Response	**Religious Leaders Response**

John 3:18

[18]Whoever believes in him is not condemned, but whoever does not believe stands condemned already because he has not believed in the name of God's one and only Son.

7. Repentance is a big deal. How does repentance reveal a proper respect for Christ's authority and an accurate understanding of oneself?

We can do the same thing. When Jesus doesn't meet our expectations, we can reject His authority in our lives. When we want terms our way, repentance is our furthest response. When we don't get our way, we can fail to embrace His mission and purpose. Jesus will also confront our sin. The question of authority is a daily choice. Will we occupy the throne of our lives, or will Christ? Surrender of self is necessary for Christ to remain in His rightful position. When we face difficult circumstances and are prone to acquiesce we can repent to re-establish Christ's rightful place in our hearts.

In order for the Pharisees to accept Christ's authority they would have to repent, believe in Christ and accept His teaching, live under His authority and embrace His purpose and mission. But they maintained they didn't need Jesus. So, they clung to their self-righteous lives like a prized possession, and left Christ where He was: rubbing shoulders with sinners, hanging out with the unlovely and sharing smiles with those who readily recognized their desperate need for forgiveness and right standing with God. The same is true for us. To fully live under the sovereign authority of Christ, our only hope is repentance. Get our faces at His feet, stop acting like we're good enough and start behaving like the One who is; accept His teaching and embrace His purpose and mission. It's time to ask ourselves an examining question. Are we living as a Pharisee, or as a follower of Christ Jesus?

Day 2: A Follower's Responsibility

The Pharisees' actions, judgments and criticisms were done in the name of God, in an effort to uphold the Law, even their rejection of Christ's authority. But, Christ was repulsed by their external show. It chills me to consider how many times I have made choices, corrected and even judged others, believing it was right according to God, only to neglect the bigger problem of my hard heart. It grieves me to acknowledge how often I have missed opportunities to lavish grace, exude mercy and offer compassion, only to prove how right I was and fail to actually realize how wrong I was.

♡ Heart Exam

1. Share a time when you did something for God only to miss the heart of the matter. Let me guess, it has probably happened more than once, huh? Me too.

As followers of Christ, we hold a tremendous responsibility. Our lives are meant to accurately appropriate Christ's redemptive power and to intimately experience His redeeming love. When we do this we will be less prone to wrongly do things in His name. When we experience His redeeming love we are painfully aware of how our sin cost Him His life. When our lives reveal His redemptive power we have no greater joy than to show others how very big our God is because of what He continues to do through us, not because of our effort, but because of His grace.

> *We cannot embrace God's passion for people without embracing His purpose for mankind: to know Christ and to make Him known.*

The Pharisees did not belong to Christ. They refused to listen and receive Him as their own. Because they rejected Him they did not know Him; they only knew about Him. In John 8:42-47, Jesus declared that because they didn't believe Christ's truth, they didn't belong to God either. ***"The reason you do not hear is that you do not belong to God"*** (v. 47). God wants to be more than an acquaintance. In order to know Christ we must receive His truth, pick up His cross, and embrace His mission to seek and save the lost.

Christ is still rejected today just as He was in the first century, but His purpose remains the same. This gives us no excuse for not joining Him in His ministry of reconciliation. We cannot accept Christ and remain tight-lipped or tightfisted about sharing Him with others. We cannot take up His cross without crucifying our own selfish desires of self-preservation, busyness and fear. We cannot embrace His passion for people without embracing His purposes for mankind: To know Christ and to make Him known; to glorify Christ and to make His glory known; to be His disciple and to disciple others; to embrace His mission and make His mission known.

There is a misconception about this business of knowing Christ and our responsibility to exude His love to others. A faulty understanding is that it will somehow be easy. Some presume that once they become a Christian all is peachy and no difficulty will come their way, as if living for Christ will come

Day 2

with no cost, no suffering and no misfortune. Clearly this is not biblical. Christ endured great suffering to proclaim His purpose (John 15:18-25). He faced tremendous opposition, even from religious leaders and those who didn't want Him known. It cost Him His life. Today is no different. His passion to reconcile mankind enabled Him to suffer because He was obediently surrendered to God's will and not His own.

The real issue is how we greet the trials we meet.

Your suffering may be different from someone's in another country, state, family or home. Let's not compare his, hers, theirs and yours. There will always be someone who has it worse off than we do. The real issue is **how** we greet the trials we meet.

2. Share some of the heartache you have experienced because you bear the name of Christ.

3. John 16:33 offers believers tremendous hope through Christ. *"I have told you these things, so that in me you will have peace. In this world you will have trouble. But take heart! I have overcome the world."* How does this verse spur you on to endure the trouble you presently face and will encounter?

To know Christ is to suffer with Him and for Him on behalf of His kingdom. Some of the greatest difficulties I have ever endured have been through painful trials at the hands of others. We grow to know God through His Word, which sustains us. But knowledge that comes through experience teaches us more about what it means to be a Christ follower. It's not until our faith is tested that we are challenged to put what we cognitively know about God and His Word into practice. For example, I could be a really great Christian if it wasn't for "them!" "They" tend to expose the ugliness that resides within us, that we may not even realize is there until we're challenged or hurt. I will be the first to confess how hard it is to love difficult individuals. But Christ did.

> One time I experienced ridicule from co-workers when I made an honest claim for all the tips I received as a waitress because their fear of the IRS auditing them was crippling. Interestingly, after a few weeks they didn't seem to need my services anymore.

There are plenty of examples and I'm sure we all have our own. Here's the point: when we live in obedient surrender to Christ, His will and His purpose; when we embrace His mission with the same fervency He had; when we grip the difficult and resist our own desires, we won't have to go look for suffering like we're at an Easter egg hunt—it will find us on its own.

Day 2

If we're not experiencing some level of discomfort in our faith, then we need to check our pulse to see if we're alive or we need re-evaluate our passion and purpose for living. In the parable of the sower, Matthew 13:20-21, Jesus teaches, *"The one who received the seed (the word of God) that fell on rocky places is the man who hears the word and at once receives it with joy. But since he has no root, he lasts only a short time. When trouble or persecution comes because of the word, he quickly falls away."* Sowing the Word of God deep within our souls enables our spiritual roots to remain anchored—regardless of impending hardship and suffering.

Something happens when we willingly lay down our will to the Father's. We become indispensable vessels who learn to graciously live when we feel ready to crack or to crumble. The gospel strengthens us to endure such trouble, in the name of Christ. We know our inheritance is not of this world, which makes suffering an experience to know Christ more intimately and to boldly show the world His glory.

Before Christ's death, many believed in Him but would not confess their faith in Him as the Messiah because they feared being thrown out of the synagogue by the Pharisees. John 12:42-43, tells us they remained silent because they loved praise from men more than praise from God. They lacked bold courage to openly express their belief in Jesus. Even in the first century there were consequences for claiming Christ as the Messiah. There are for us, too.

John 12:42-43

[42]Yet at the same time many even among the leaders believed in him. But because of the Pharisees they would not confess their faith for fear they would be put out of the synagogue; [43]for they loved praise from men more than praise from God.

We have to choose how bold we will be in our faith. If we quietly follow and never openly share our faith we may need to take some personal inventory. We may need to consider what we are afraid of and who we are trying to please. Please don't misunderstand when I say "bold." I'm not talking about being belligerent and disrespectful towards people, but rather having a firm conviction of love for our Savior and a willingness to share Him with others, regardless, and with the knowledge we may not be received. The American culture does not tolerate Christians, but we should always be ready to give to others an account of our faith in love.

4. Describe your level of courage to live boldly for Christ. How do your fears inhibit you?

The Pharisees quieted people's belief in Christ. Often, we too are derailed when praise from men carries more weight than praise from God. Who hushes your love for Him? Ask God to give you courage to face the necessary consequences of your obedient expression.

5. How can our level of boldness be related to our level of suffering?

Day 2

Read Acts 4:1-22

6. Verses 17-20 are intriguing. Have you ever been in a situation similar to Peter and John's? Describe your situation and share your response and outcome.

7. How does the example of Peter and John motivate you to courageously speak about what you have experienced in Christ?

After Christ's death and ascension the disciples were unwavering in their faith. In Acts, Peter and John are told to stop preaching about Christ. The Sanhedrin feared this message would spread so they strived to suppress any effort of its growth. Christ's disciples were bold. They spoke with great courage because they knew the truth of Christ *and* they knew they possessed the life-changing gospel message available to all who would believe.

Suppress the gospel at all costs. Really? This is what our culture would have us do. We possess the source of light and life, but men love the darkness. It should come as no surprise to us when people try to squelch our faith. In truth, they're not rejecting us, but rather Christ. He forewarned us of what we were to expect as His followers. Rejection and suffering is what we signed up for the day we accepted Him as Lord.

Read Luke 19:37-40

This scene touches my heart. It is the final week of Christ's life. Similar to King Solomon's entry at his presentation as the king to Jerusalem (1 Kings 1:33-46), Christ enters Jerusalem on a donkey for His official entry as Messiah and King of all Kings. He enters the city on the day when people are picking their lamb to be slain for Passover. In reality, Christ's triumphal procession is the presentation of Himself—as the once-for-all Passover Lamb.[1] Christ's followers welcome Him accordingly.

1 *The One Year Book of Christian History by E. Michael & Sharon Rusten. Tyndale House Publishers, © 2003. p. 180-181.*

Day 2

The Pharisees on guard duty are quick to sharpen their pointy fingers. They audaciously tell Christ to rebuke His disciples because they were joyfully praising God in loud voices as they quoted Psalm 118:26a. Jesus puts them in their place. *"If they keep quiet the rocks will cry out."* Friends, the rocks will cry out indeed. The rocks will cry out if our praises don't.

Consider the following:

- † We cannot hush what deserves honor.
- † We cannot recoil at what should be revered.
- † We cannot suppress what should be shouted.
- † We cannot conceal what should be celebrated.
- † We cannot stifle what should be esteemed.
- † We cannot muzzle what should be magnified.
- † We must boldly proclaim our Beloved King!

Psalm 118:26a

Blessed is he who comes in the name of the Lord.

When we serve God and not men, we need to expect opposition. When our lives demonstrate exuberant faith it will begin to mess with people. Some may be convicted because it exposes their hypocritical lives. Others will be drawn to it because an authentic expression of devotion to Christ is something they have yet to see. Either way, our responsibility as a follower of Christ is the same. And never forget, the rocks will cry out if we don't.

Day 3: Woes & Warnings

This study has addressed specific faults of the Pharisees and teachers of the Law. Although we have reviewed different accounts throughout the Gospels, many of them are captured in two lengthy sections of Scripture: Matthew 23 and Luke 11. Jesus indicts the religious leaders with seven woes. He pinpoints different areas of hypocrisy, addresses what they should have done and warns them of coming judgment and accountability for their sin.

Jesus' rebuke is stern. This isn't exactly a nice three-point Father's Day sermon about why they should feel good about themselves. It's more like a seven-point lashing before His journey to the cross. Jesus wasn't out to make friends; He was out to minister the truth of the kingdom of God. We must consider the first-century mindset of the people and the implications of the religious leaders' false teaching. Christ had to correct their wrongs so the people would no longer be led astray and kept from the Kingdom. Up to this time the people only knew the Law according to the interpretation of the Pharisees. As we've clearly seen, Christ fiercely opposes their heresy and hypocrisy concerning the Law. He confronts them publicly with a listening crowd and His disciples present. Christ wants to make sure the Pharisees aren't the only ones witnessing His reprimand. Let's take a look at the woes before we get to Christ's warnings.

Read Matthew 23 (Cross reference Luke 11:39-52)

1. Summarize the seven woes Christ admonishes the religious leaders for.

2. What words does Jesus use to describe them? What is the main description He uses for them?

3. What present-day "woes" would Jesus reprove you for? Fill in the blank, "Woe to you________"

I know we've already answered similar questions to the last one during this study, but truthfully we could have dealt with pride in Week Two, greed in Week Three, hypocrisy in Week Four and now find ourselves battling pride again this week. The human heart is wild and precocious, nursing old sins until the battle in our hearts is won again and again. I know this full well because I was faced *again* this week with, *"Woe to you Hester, for you are being selfish, greedy and propelled by wrong motives."* I am a weak woman and am bothered by this. Oh for Christ, who cleanses my unloving heart. I know I have the propensity for these sins but I was, you know, feeling pretty good about things, and then, wham! To my knees I go again.

Heart Exam

4. How are you reconciling the reproofs Jesus has for you? How is your heart responding?

5. Take a moment to read Matthew 5:3-9. Contrast the first seven blessings Jesus announces for His true disciples compared to the seven woes listed in question 1. I think it's safe to say we would rather receive blessings over curses wouldn't we?

Before Jesus specifically disputes the Pharisees in His entourage of criticisms, He gives an adamant warning to those who have ears to hear:

- Don't do what they [Pharisees] do (Matthew 23:3).
- Be on your guard against their hypocrisy (Luke 12:1b).

Jesus warns others because the Pharisees don't practice what they preach. And others are not to do what they do. These religious leaders sat in Moses' seat as the formative authority on matters pertaining to the Law. Remember, the Law was delivered through Moses. Whether this seat was actually present in synagogues or not, it can also metaphorically refer to a place from which experts on the law taught. [1] The disciples were expected to obey these religious leaders insofar as they accurately interpreted the Law. And, they were to abide by the Law of Moses, but not the burdensome additions these leaders included. As we've already learned, Jesus made it quite evident how their extra biblical traditions and teachings were wrong.

1 *ESV Study Bible. Crossway Bibles, © 2008. p. 1870.*

Day 3

In Luke 12:1b, Jesus alerted His disciples to be on guard against the yeast of the Pharisees. We are to take heed and beware of this yeast because of its danger and potential destruction. Matthew 16:11-12 also describes another aspect of this yeast.

6. What was the yeast of the Pharisees? Why would it have been necessary for the disciples to guard against this?

> *Matthew 16:11-12*
>
> *[11]How is it you don't understand that I was not talking to you about bread? But be on your guard against the yeast of the Pharisees and Sadducees." [12]Then they understood that he was not telling them to guard against the yeast used in bread, but against the teaching of the Pharisees and Sadducees.*

7. How has this contagious yeast infiltrated your life? And, how do you see the impact of this on others around you? (Think of what yeast does to fresh bread dough. It only takes a little to spread throughout the whole batch.)

8. How can you practically be on guard against the yeast of the Pharisees?

> *"Nowhere does Jesus appear more like an OT prophet than in Matt. 23. He called the Pharisees back to the 'weightier matters of the law' (23:23). He called them to close the gap between their profession and their performance. It is because they were so close (and yet so far) from being what they ought to have been and yet at the same time made a great fuss over their supposed accomplishments (cf. Lk. 18:11), that Jesus took them to task in such ominous tones."* [2]

Hypocrisy and false teaching are lethal toxins for anyone claiming Christ. What we practice must match what we preach. Saying one thing and doing another, or expecting of someone else what we don't do ourselves, communicates a gospel that has yet to penetrate the depths of our depraved hearts. Are we emulating the qualities of our High Priest or that of a pagan?

Jesus didn't tolerate hypocrisy and false teaching in the first century and He certainly doesn't accept it in the twenty-first century either. As Luke 11:28 echoes shortly before Jesus' "woe" discourse, ***"Blessed rather are those who hear the word of God and obey it."*** May we live what we teach and practice what we preach. And, let's never forget those three powerful words that should reverberate through our minds, "Woe to you . . . "

2 *The Zondervan Encyclopedia of the Bible, Vol 4. Merrill C. Tenney, General Editor, Zondervan, Grand Rapids, MI @2009. p. 842-852.*

Day 4: Practice What You Preach

The tail end of yesterday's lesson introduces the main focus for today, practicing what we preach. The world judges Christians because they accuse them of being hypocrites, and rightly so. We're all hypocrites in some form or another. Without trying to minimize spiritual hypocrisy, I believe the real rub comes when Christians are not willing to admit they struggle and fail. We all do. But, some of us are better at covering it up than others. The bitterness the world tastes is when we won't admit our weaknesses and instead pretend we don't have them. This misrepresents the gospel and offers no hope to outsiders because we're all messed up, unable to fix ourselves on our own.

When we are authentic with others we can graciously tell them we are a Christian and acknowledge Christ's redemptive power, His continual transformation and our constant need of His grace and presence. It's a whole lot easier to practice what we preach when we remain aware of our constant need of Christ's atonement. This reality enables God's power to exude through us. This is when we recognize we are hopeless without Him and He empowers us to overcome our hang-ups. But, even when we do falter, we surrender again to His righteousness and exchange our sin for more of Him.

Heart Exam

1. When is it most difficult for you to practice what you preach?

2. How willing are you to share your weaknesses with others?

Why is practicing what we preach incredibly difficult for some and not for others? I consider my own life and the painfully humbling moments when God rebukes me and then gently restores. I have also gleaned biblical truths from the lives of the Pharisees and I'm left with an answer I believe is foundational to this problem. Sometimes, we don't practice what we preach because we fail to live what we believe. The world's judgment upon Christians is that the chasm stretches too far—our lives don't profess what our mouths confess.

A profession of faith is futile without any tangible results. Seeking God's holiness will inspire us to embrace authenticity because we accept we cannot truly reflect His holiness without stripping ourselves of hypocrisy. Pursuing God's holiness also implies we cannot accept Christ without experiencing changed lives. Our gratitude compels us to live differently.

Day 4

Like the Pharisees, we can have lots of knowledge about God and the Bible but not have a relationship with Christ. An intimate fellowship with Jesus sinks into our core and leaves us changed. Many people score well on religious knowledge tests but still have hearts far from the Father. Many people can say they believe in Christ but even the demons can do that (James 2:19; Mark 3:11; 5:7). Knowledge of God is useless unless it transforms the way we believe, which will influence the way we live.

> *Mark 3:11*
>
> *11 Whenever the evil spirits saw him, they fell down before him and cried out, "You are the Son of God."*

Truth is, knowing something is different from believing in something. Knowledge is not enough—it doesn't require commitment. When we believe in something it changes the way we live. We will act upon our beliefs. Our lives validate what we truly believe because our beliefs influence and impact our behavior. Living what we say we believe changes us from the inside out.

Our faith is defined by what we do. The word for faith and belief come from the same Greek root word, *pistis*. Its verb form, *pisteuo* means to be persuaded of or to place confidence in something. It is more than credence; it is reliance. [1] Intellectual assent is not sufficient.

The book of James is written to Christians: those who had already accepted justification by faith. The problem is that those he is writing to weren't living up to what they professed. In essence, James tells them, "*You say you believe in Christ . . . well show me.*" Let's see what James has to say about faith—how he defines biblical faith and what this looks like.

Read James 2:14-26

James shows us three kinds of faith. The first, shown in verse 20, is foolish faith, where we 'talk it.' ***"You foolish man, do you want evidence that faith without deeds is useless. In the same way, faith by itself, if it is not accompanied by action, is dead"*** (v. 17). Foolish faith believes that faith doesn't need deeds. People like this might know the right Christian lingo, but their talk doesn't reach any further than their lips. This kind of faith substitutes words for deeds. He shares a practical example of a Christian telling his naked and starved sibling, "*Go, I wish you well,*" without aiding him, showing that this man's faith isn't active. The metaphor of the dead body James uses is to teach that this kind of faith is dead, without life. Our faith is as good as a cadaver if we believe we can have faith without action. Essentially, foolish faith is dead faith.

The second kind of faith, shown in verse19, is intellectual faith or mental assent, where we "think it." ***"You believe there is one God. Good! Even the demons believe that—and shudder."*** Mental assent is given to the right facts and information about Christ, but faith is not just an intellectual understanding of who Christ is. Knowledge is not enough. Remember, knowledge doesn't require commitment. What irony. The demons had knowledge of God but did not place their faith in Him.

---

1 Vines Expository Dictionary by W.E. Vine. Thomas Nelson Publishers, ©1996.

3. What good is a profession of faith without any change of life? What truth is in empty words?

4. What benefit is knowledge of God alone?

The third kind of faith James addresses, in verse 14, is obedient faith. Obedient faith is saving faith. This is when we "live it." *"What good is it my brothers, if a man claims to have faith but has no deeds? Can such faith save him?"* This suggests there *is* a faith that saves. Saving faith leads us to an obedient response where we express and demonstrate what we believe. This happens in our faith walk when we not only "talk it" and "think it," but we "live it"!

This is what I call the foundational trio: Information, transformation and application. These three pillars are necessary components in our relationship with God. Information enters our heads—where cognitive understanding takes place. Then it penetrates our hearts—where transformation occurs. And finally it is lived out in our lives—where application is seen. When these three components are not combined and exercised together there is a gaping spiritual disconnect regarding the gospel's effect in our lives.

5. What does James 2:21-24 say made Abraham's faith complete?

6. What is the biblical teaching regarding faith and deeds according to the above passage? How does this resonate with your walk?

Day 4

If there is no action as a result of our faith in Christ, then it's not faith because we are not putting full confidence in what we understand to be true. If there is no demonstration of our beliefs then our beliefs are not true beliefs. Or, we are not being true to our beliefs. This means we probably do not really believe what we say we do. If we genuinely believe, it will reveal itself because this is the nature of faith. Faith is defined by what we demonstrate. How we live tells others what we believe. When information transforms our hearts, applying the gospel to our lives is a tangible result. When this occurs, the dark and dying world we inhabit will accurately see the light and life of Christ in us and through us, causing them to be drawn to His presence, rather than repelled by His followers' hypocrisy.

Day 5: Internal and External Purity

It hardly seems possible this is the final lesson for this six-week study. I pray it has been a productive journey as we have dug deeper into God's Word and into our hearts. As mentioned in Week One, Day 1, the condition of one's heart is the basis for a relationship with God. When it is contaminated or misaligned the fruit of our life will match accordingly. Keeping our heart's soil fertile for the seed of His truth, weeding when the flesh seeks to sprout, and daily submission to the Gardner will ensure continual growth through the Lord's cultivation.

At the beginning of this study I shared how the Lord sowed the seed for this project to take place. As I prepared message material for a conference several years ago I was haunted by Jesus' words in Matthew 5:20, *"For I tell you that unless your righteousness surpasses that of the Pharisees and teachers of the law, you will certainly not enter the kingdom of heaven."*

This truth pierced my soul. I was hungry to learn more so I could prevent my own heart from resembling theirs. We inhibit our relationship with Christ when we live pious lives. When our righteousness stems from self and promotes self, we position ourselves above Christ. When our righteousness comes through Christ we are submitted to His position over us. We must continually reject the temptation to be justified by our performance and embrace that Christ's glory and righteousness shines through us when His payment for our sin is embedded within us.

Read John 7:45-49

The Pharisees snap at the temple guards and insist they have been deceived by Jesus and declare the people present are out of line.

1. What do the Pharisees proclaim in verse 49?

____

____

____

____

The irony in this passage is that the Pharisees pronounce their own judgment. They are the ones who really don't understand the Law, and the curse actually falls on them because of this.

The Pharisees' righteousness hung on strict adherence to their self-imposed additions to the Mosaic Law. But Jesus taught in Matthew 22:40 that, *"All the Law and the Prophets hang on these two commandments."* Which two? First, love God. Secondly, love others. The basis of the Law was love not legalism. In essence, the Pharisees let the Law become their god, which can easily happen when we take love out of obedience.

Galatians 5:6 confirms this by teaching the only thing that counts is faith expressed through love. This kind of *agape* love shows the right attitudes and actions towards others. Wrong attitudes and actions do not come from *agape* love. In truth, what we do externally must be motivated by faith and

Day 5

agape love. If it's not, it doesn't count or have any value. Faith expressing itself through love is the spiritual equation for internal purity. When our faith is shown through love, our external actions stem from pure motives.

But sometimes we subscribe to the wrong gospel. Let me explain. We can either subscribe to the gospel of grace as a follower of Christ or the gospel of good works as a follower of the Pharisees. Christ established a new covenant through His death. Jesus set us free from the ceremonial regulations of the Law (Galatians 5:1), but not from obedience to God's moral law (Galatians 5:13-6:1). Freedom from the Law empowers believers to live by faith in the Spirit and to be motivated by love.

In the book of Galatians the apostle Paul opposes the infiltrating false teaching that insisted circumcision was necessary for salvation. He refutes the requirements of the Mosaic Law as providing justification. Paul insists that Christ's gospel is grace and love. But this gospel of works was poisoning their faith, so he had to reestablish the Galatians' spiritual foundation back to Christ and not the Law.

Paul teaches an allegory from the Old Testament with Abraham's two sons, Ishmael and Isaac. If you're not acquainted with this story please read Genesis chapters 16, 17 and 21.

2. Froms Galatians 4:21-31 list separately the descriptions and outcomes of the slave sons of Abraham versus the free sons of Abraham.

slave sons	free sons
______________	______________
______________	______________
______________	______________
______________	______________
______________	______________
______________	______________

Heart Exam

3. Which son are you and how do these blessings impact your walk with Christ?

____

____

____

____

Ishmael, the son of the slave woman Hagar, was born according to the flesh or human will when Abraham and Sarah took matters into their own hands. Isaac, the son of the free woman Sarah, was born according to a promise, and was a miraculous birth given the conditions of their physical bodies. Paul emphasizes the Galatians are from Isaac, and they too, like Isaac, are God's children by His gracious power, not according to the flesh or human effort. Similar to Ishmael persecuting Isaac (Genesis 21:9), now these Jewish teachers seeking justification by works are persecuting the Galatian Christians who accepted God's promise of justification by faith. The implication for those who teach the gospel of works is for them to be removed and no longer corrupt the true gospel of grace. [1]

4. From Galatians 5:1-6, compare and contrast justification by faith in Christ and justification through the Law.

Christ	**Law**
______	______
______	______
______	______
______	______
______	______
______	______

5. How are you seeking justification and how does this impact your relationship with Christ?

______
______
______
______

Galatians 3:10-11

[10]All who rely on observing the law are under a curse, for it is written: "Cursed is everyone who does not continue to do everything written in the Book of the Law." [11]Clearly no one is justified before God by the law, because, "The righteous will live by faith."

Paul urges them to stand firm and not submit to the yoke of slavery the Old Testament Law requires. He knows if they insist on even one part of the Law, circumcision in this case, it is then necessary for them to obey all of the Law perfectly for their justification, which is simply something they cannot do (Galatians 3:10,11,21). Because of this, Paul says, if they do enforce circumcision then Christ is of no advantage to them. He goes on to teach they cannot embrace both grace and works. For those who once accepted justification by faith and who now accept justification by the Law must not possess a relationship with Christ because they have fallen from the grace offered and available to them. [2] Even though Paul's opponents tried to teach how righteousness could be attained by human effort, he reminds the Galatians their righteousness is fulfilled only through Christ, not themselves. And, the gospel message teaches them to live by the law of Christ, which is by His Spirit, not by the Mosaic Law.

The gospel of good works assumes all our good behavior helps to appease God's wrath, like we somehow partner with Him in our salvation. When we accept this teaching we are saying Christ's blood is not enough to cover our sin, and instead, our behavior contributes to His mercy and salvation. NO! *"For it is by grace you have been saved, not by works so that no man may boast"* (Ephesians 2:8-9).

1 *ESV Study Bible. Crossway Bibles, © 2008. p. 2252-2253.*
2 *Ibid.*

Day 5

You say, *"Sure I've accepted my salvation as God's free gift of grace."* Good. But do you live under His grace or under your good works? This is fundamental to our faith and we can't accept both. When we do not live under the gospel of grace we are no longer motivated by faith characterized by love and empowered by the Holy Spirit. When this is the case, it becomes easier to look at others' lives and compare our junk to theirs, *"Well, thank goodness I'm not like them . . . Don't you know her story? . . . Whew! I'm glad I've never done that . . . etc."* And, we can look around at others and think they're not doing their part. We become quick to judge their lives and service to God.

Trying to justify ourselves by comparing our life to someone else's is not uncommon. We've all done this and may periodically be tempted. Our sin may be different from others', but if we believe our sin doesn't have the same stench in the nostrils of God, we are mistaken and don't accurately understand the Gospel of Jesus Christ.

6. How have you tried to justify your life by comparing yourself to someone else?

When we live under our good works we try to maintain something that is given as a gift. This is where the world rubs us and we retract at showing any flaws and revealing God's glory because we're too busy striving to save face. Because we're working for it, we are in bondage to keeping track of how good we think we are, *and* desperately want others to notice our righteous life. If our mentality keeps score for the good we do, we are held captive to obligation and works-based righteousness. We should not live like a trophy case on wheels, showing all our great contents, accomplishments and luster. This is hypocrisy at its finest.

When we live under the gospel of grace we readily recognize our sin for what it is. We acknowledge we are hopeless without Christ's atoning blood and we view others as Christ would—in need of His grace too. We no longer view others' sins categorically or measure them by human standards. We see others through the Kingdom lens, as God's beloved children, and our hearts are then compelled to minister His grace to them.

This isn't saying we won't do good works, because in truth we are created to do them (Ephesians 2:10). Our purpose and motivation, however, should be changed from duty to gratitude. When we feel obligated to do things we fail to embrace the gospel of grace. When grace takes hold of our hearts we are driven to serve God and evangelize His truth because our gratefulness for His grace overflows from our lives.

We already know the Pharisees liked to keep track of their good works and made sure others knew. It's obvious when we read the New Testament. We can easily point a finger and accuse them for not getting it, when all the while we may be doing the same thing. We make sure others know what we don't do or stand against . . . to the fault they often don't know what we do stand for. The gospel of grace changes everything because it is motivated by love—God's love. Then we become willing to reveal our weaknesses to others. This shows them the hope of Christ and the ability to overcome in His name, by His power. If we are living under the gospel of good works it's time to repent because it is NOT the Gospel of Christ.

7. How does subscribing to the gospel of good works contribute to a hypocritical life?

8. How does living under God's grace encourage a non-hypocritical life?

9. Which gospel do you live under? How do you know?

When we live our lives based on good works our faith won't penetrate any deeper than our hands, unlike a life based on God's grace where our faith punctures our hearts. What will impact the world are those with authentic faith, evidenced by how they live under God's grace by His Spirit. Those who seek to earn spiritual service certificates and trophy case righteousness will always miss THE point of the gospel. We must live under the gospel of grace, motivated by faith, characterized by love and empowered by the Holy Spirit.

We must live under the gospel of grace, motivated by faith, characterized by love and empowered by the Holy Spirit.

> *"Pharisaism was at heart, thought tragically miscarried, a movement for RIGHTEOUSNESS. It was this concern for righteousness that drove the Pharisees to their own self-satisfaction, and unknowingly they rejected their only hope of righteousness."* [3]

Do you remember in Week Two when you were asked to write down all of the resumé items you could boast about and falsely take righteousness in? I pleaded with you to be detailed and that you would find out why later. Well friends, later is now. Take a moment and go back to Week Two, Day 4 (page 50) and review your answer to this question and please add anything new

3 *The Zondervan Encyclopedia of the Bible, Vol* 4. Merrill C. Tenney, General Editor, Zondervan, Grand Rapids, MI @2009. p. 842-852.

that comes to your mind. Now, please take the time to write these additional items on a separate piece of paper. I know this may be time consuming but please complete this exercise.

Finally, find a quiet place to be alone. Position your heart before His throne of grace. Humbly confess, one at a time, each of those items you have boasted in. Seek the Lord's forgiveness and grace to embrace His righteousness. Confidently express your eagerness to live Christlike in a counterfeit culture, to possess internal purity over external piety and for His Spirit to gently warn you when your flesh desires the opposite. When you are finished praying, you may burn, tear or destroy your resumé of righteousness as you wish and may it ever depart from your heart.

My greatest prayer for this entire study is that we would tattoo on our hearts the truth that God desires to purify them—for us to live with internal purity over external piety. This occurs when our external actions are motivated by pure internal intentions. As we've learned, we can strive for externally right behavior and still possess an internally wrong heart. Spiritual agreement and maturity transpires when pure external actions are the result from pure internal motives based on faith expressed through love. And, when we are truly internally pure, we will also be externally genuine. Friends, this is when our righteousness will indeed exceed that of the Pharisees and teachers of the Law. This will also be when we live Christlike in a counterfeit culture.

Day 5

PHARISEE'S PURITY PRAYER

Merciful, Gracious and Sovereign Lord, I humbly seek a pure heart:

Grant me grace over judgment
Give me Your glory, not mine

I ask You to ...
Purge my performance
Relinquish my rote rituals
Lance any legalism
Penetrate my pride
Compel me to compassion
Purify my motives

May I ...
Heed humility
Fast because of freedom
Give out of gratitude
Rest through Your righteousness
Magnify Your mercy
Multiply Your grace

I choose to ...
Submit my stubborn will to You
Worship You without worry
Contend for the gospel, not pretend
Rub shoulders with sinners, not only the "saved"
Live Kingdom-driven versus self-driven
Renounce my resume' of righteousness

Please help me to ...
Honor my heritage in Christ
Love without limits
Replace confidence in the flesh with confidence in the cross
Live as a follower of Christ, not a Pharisee
Embrace internal purity instead of external piety
Live Christlike in a counterfeit culture

In Jesus' mighty and holy name,
Amen.

Psalm 42:1; Ephesians 6:17; Hebrews 4:12; 2 Timothy 3:16; Deuteronomy 32:47

Know God / Know about God -

The goal of our Christian lives is not merely information, but rather ______________________ .

• •

Know *(oida)* – communicates to know anything; to get knowledge or understanding; to discern, discover, observe; to understand as fact. This word occurs 335 times in the New Testament - (1 John 5:13; James 4:4; Matthew 9:6). [1]

Know *(ginosko)* – means to learn to know; perceive, feel; and it communicates knowledge coming from ____________. This word occurs 225 times in the New Testament (John 14:7; 17). [2]

(Oida) communicates ____________ assent and the other, *(ginosko)*, reveals intimate __________________ with God.

• •

Know God's Written Word –

† The foundation for knowing God's Word needs to stem from the right motivation – to prepare ourselves to live transformed lives, not to impress others with our __________________ .

1. Delight in His Word – Attitude and perspective make a big difference. When we approach God's Word as an ________________ instead of duty, our relationship with Him will thrive.

2. Invested in His Word –

3. Mature with time – When God's Word is not consistently penetrating our hearts we are likely to become more ________- ________________ and less God-dependent. We will also have a lot less resolve when we're faced with ______________________ .

4. Equipped for life --

"God hands you lungs when He hands you His Word. Steep in Scripture, and it's like carrying your own oxygen tank." Ann Voskamp [3]

Deuteronomy 32:47 "These are not idle words. These are your __________ ."

Costume or uniform? A costume ____________ .

A uniform ____________ .

Special Thanks

My wonderful husband, David: You are a constant source of encouragement and love. Thank you for your leadership in my life and our home. I could not serve as I do without your support and blessing. I love serving the Lord with you. My three loving sons, Tucker, Spencer, and Cooper, you always have kind words and high-fives to offer as I tackle new ministry projects. You are all a delight.

Elvina Green, you were the first to invite me teach at women's Bible study at CFCC. Your faithful discipleship of me and your challenge to love the Word of God and love Jesus has stuck with me. Jannica Johnson, your phone call in the spring of 2007 to join the women's teaching team at ECC. Kristy Lenhardt, your phone call in the spring of 2010 to write a Bible study. These three invitations planted the seeds and ignited the flames God used to formally propel me forward in writing, teaching, and speaking. Each of you have been a pillar of unwavering strength and support. I will never forget the impact you have all made in my life.

Carol Stine, Kristy Lenhardt, Jannica Johnson, Lisa Johnston, Carrie Cook, Mandy Kenney, Megan Osborne, Martha Hightower, Linda Jackson: My dear ECC sisters who partnered together for the Kingdom. For your commitment to count all things loss compared to the surpassing greatness of knowing Christ, your uncompromising passion to hide God's Word in your hearts, and your desire to disciple others in His truth. Thank you for inviting and initiating the opportunity to unleash and utilize my gifts, for recognizing and affirming God's work in me, for your endearing love, encouragement and supportive embrace. You are all instruments of righteousness in the hands of God. I hold you very close to my heart. And special thanks to the pilot group who went through this study as a small group. Your insight and feedback has strengthened its effectiveness. Glory to God!

My family, Gabe & Rhiannon, Joya, Uncle Randy & Aunt Joy, my faithful college friends and my remarkable prayer team: Your exhortations of love, your interest and inquiry and your commitment to pray for me these past several years has greatly ministered to my heart. It blesses me to know you lift my needs before His throne. You are precious gifts.

To the special women of Valley Real Life: Since our move to Spokane, many of you have played a significant role in seeking me out to offer your warm embrace and support. Your affirmation, prayers and blessing have been a reflection to me of Christ's love. Thank you for lifting my heart on discouraging days, for offering help and for your joyful reception of me into the body of Christ at VRL.

VRL Tuesday AM Ladies 2013/2014: You are a treasure. Your desire to know God and your hunger for His Word is a testimony to your love for Him. Thank you for the privilege to serve you and for the blessing to teach you this study as the inaugural group. May our journey toward Christlikeness be a constant source of joy.

Sam & Shayla McGhee, Elliott & Tiffany Wallach, Ethan Moss, and Sue Overland: Your willingness to partner with me in your areas of gifting speaks volumes regarding your passion and heart to advance God's Kingdom. Your talents are apparent and it is a joy to collaborate with you in the design, layout, and videography details of this project. God bless each of you for your many hours of sacrifice and service to minister to others to the glory of God. I am humbled by your gracious outpouring of love. "Thank you" hardly expresses my depth of gratitude.

My Lord and Savior, Jesus Christ. Thank you for loving an insecure, prideful, judgmental woman as I. Without the transforming power of Your Holy Spirit I would still be drowning in people-pleasing, perfection, and performance. I praise You for replacing my heart of stone. May my testimony serve as a witness to the all-surpassing greatness of knowing You. My deepest prayer is that You are glorified through this project. Thank you, Lord, for inspiring this work and for sustaining me through its completion. Soli Deo Gloria!

ENDNOTES

The following resources were also used as research material in the course of writing this Bible study:

Week One

Achtemeirt, Paul J. (1989), *Harper's Bible Dictionary,* Harper San Francisco Publishing (p. 782-783).
ESV Study Bible, Crossway Bibles, Wheaton, Illinois 2008 p. 217, 221, 2068, 2297, 2409.
Hale, Thomas (1996) *The Applied New Testament Commentary,* Chariot Victor Publishing (p. 197, 212).
Matthew Henry Complete Commentary on the Whole Bible [online] Available http://www.studylight.org/com/mhc-com/view.cgi?book=lu&chapter=007 (November 30, 2012).
Tenney, Merrill C. (1967), *Pictorial Bible Dictionary,* Zondervan Publishers (p. 204, 739).
The Adam Clarke Commentary [online] Available http://www.studylight.org/com/acc/view.cgi?book=lu&chapter=007 (November 30, 2012).

viewer guide *(pg 31)*

1 http://classic.studylight.org/isb/view.cgi?number=1125, (1-8-2014).
2 http://classic.studylight.org/isb/view.cgi?number=5055 (1-8-2014).
3 http://classic.studylight.org/isb/view.cgi?number=5498 (1-8-2014).
http://www3.telus.net/public/kstam/en/temple/details/priest_service.htm (1-8-2014).
http://crossward.org/bullsandgoats (1-8-2014).
http://www.biblestudytools.com/dictionary/scourging/ (1-15-2014).
http://www.keyway.ca/htm2000/20000905.htm (1-15-2014).

Week Three

http://www.gty.org/blog/B110908?term=servants%20of%20a%20new%20covenant (1-25-14).

viewer guide *(pg 81)*

1 http://classic.studylight.org/isb/view.cgi?number=1401 (1-25-14).
2 *ESV Study Bible,* Crossway Bibles, Wheaton, Illinois. ©2008, p.177-178.

Week Four

viewer guide *(pg 105)*

1 http://classic.studylight.org/isb/view.cgi?number=1249 (2-3-2014).
2 http://classic.studylight.org/isb/view.cgi?number=1401 (2-3-2014).

Week five

Crane, Steven A. (2010) *Marveling With Mark*, Wipf & Stock (p. 45-53).

viewer guide *(pg 129)*

1 http://classic.studylight.org/isb/view.cgi?number=25 (2-10-2014).
2 http://classic.studylight.org/isb/view.cgi?number= 3650 (2-10-2014).
3 http://classic.studylight.org/isb/view.cgi?number= 2588 (2-10-2014).
4 http://classic.studylight.org/isb/view.cgi?number= 5590 (2-10-2014).
5 http://classic.studylight.org/isb/view.cgi?number= 1271 (2-10-2014).
6 http://classic.studylight.org/isb/view.cgi?number= 2479 (2-10-2014).

Week Six

viewer guide *(pg 154)*

1 http://www.blueletterbible.org/lang/lexicon/lexicon.cfm?Strongs=G6063 =NASB.
2 http://www.blueletterbible.org/lang/lexicon/lexicon.cfm?Strongs= G1097=NASB.
3 http://www.aholyexperience.com/2013/01/the-1-habit-god-really-wants-for-your-new-year/January 24, 2013 blog post quote:

Made in the USA
Columbia, SC
08 April 2025